CLIENTS? WHO WANTS THEM? I DO!!

This book is written by an octogenarian, who has spent 65 years in the Accountancy profession and offers an insight into an Accountants' public practice in 1950s and 1960s and 1970s when H M Treasury and the profession had a mutual respect for each other, which has now deteriorated. Some of the unusual Clients cases are examined with humour and understanding.

The writer has used an assumed name as he is still in part time practice not only for the enjoyment he receives but also to add to the meager income he receives from the Government.

CLIENTS? WHO WANTS THEM? I DO!!

Peregrine St John

CLIENTS? WHO WANTS THEM? I DO!!

Olympia Publishers
London

www.olympiapublishers.com
OLYMPIA PAPERBACK EDITION

A CIP catalogue record for this title is
available from the British Library.

ISBN: 978-1-905513-74-1

First Published in 2008

Olympia Publishers
60 Cannon Street
London
EC4N 6NP

Printed in Great Britain

DEDICATION

To Max and Dawn for their help and dedication,
and to Katie and Betsy
for their support and encouragement.
And to the late Diana
For all of these

****

As this is my first book, I wish to give grateful
thanks to my publishers: Olympia Publishers,
particularly to Gina, Sarah, and all the
editors for their help and support.

POTTED BIOGRAPHY

The author of this book has used a *nome de plume*. He was born in the 1920's, a time of deprivation and turmoil. The General Strike and a few years later, the Wall Street crash, created a period of financial upheaval.

His father was a gentlemen's tailor and mother a tailoress and dressmaker. Although times were difficult and money was short, they gave him a loving and caring home, without the author being aware of their difficulties. They, in their wisdom, gave him the opportunities they never had, by not kidnapping him for the workshop they had to endure in their youth. They supported him with encouragement and finance during his studies for his chosen profession, and in his endeavors.

During the Second World War, most London schools were closed due to the evacuation to the safer areas for the children, the author returned to his junior school – as he had not left the city. The Head informed him that he should teach mathematics to the few children still attending, which he did until age thirteen when he took his first employment as a clerk to a large armament manufacturing company. After two years, the author was introduced to a practicing accountant and began studying for the profession. After a few changes of employers, the author decided in 1948 to commence full-time practice as an accountant and continued full-time until 1988. Since then, he has a part-time practice and responsibility as a Financial Controller to several companies.

The author has broadcast in the past on local radio on various topics and has reported and edited membership magazines. His interests are his family, sports – particularly cricket where he is a member of the M.C.C. (The Marlebone Cricket Club) and golf, where his handicap is *golf*. He is interested in flying and aircraft, particularly the First World War and is presently researching and will eventually write a pamphlet of certain World War flyers.

He feels that the world is full of humour and is dedicated in searching for it.

INTRODUCTION

In another time and another place this diary recounts some anecdotal episodes and recollections of ordinary folk. We'll never again see these days and events. Therefore to capture these moments in, yes, good old-fashioned print, it becomes essential reading and dare I be so bold to say, of historical interest.

Contents

Chapter 1

IT'S ALL ABOUT THE PERCEPTION

I had an Accountancy Practice. The fact that accountants arc considered 'nerds' – unattractive, humourless, stick-in-the muds, unworldly and every word in the dictionary for 'dull and boring' will create a thunderous clap of thunder as hundred thousand (if I'm lucky), or probably twenty copies of this book are slammed shut.

But, I plead dear reader, to persevere, as you will probably find later that the cases I have dealt with over many years are of some interest.

We are probably all of the above, but it is our clients that hold the attention. They are our mainstay. They pay our fees and to whom we must show respect, as they do to us. In the grand past days of our profession, our clients treated us with the respect they thought we deserved, for our professionalism and education. To see their solicitor[*], bank manager or accountant, in most instances, they would wear their 'Sunday Best'[†] and almost touch their forelocks in deference to our so-called exalted position. Appointments were made with certain

---

[*] Lawyer
[†] Finest Suit

17

trepidation, apprehension and an amount of civility. Nowadays, the client is in casual clothes, late for meetings, telephone, fax, email and text for immediate answers, whether it be at night or weekends and holidays. The new recruits to the profession take this as the norm. They know no better, poor souls! Times do change, and I do not wish to countenance the present. We are all experts in our own fields, whether we are professional or as they used to say: 'in trade'.[*]

In my professional career – such as it was – I had two main employers, then known as principals. To lighten the tale, my second was the absolute antipathy of my first, who was known by his staff and all that know him as a bastard of the first order. Unfortunately you'll hear more of him later – although a book could have been written about him alone. We will start with the good guy as a comparison, to wet the appetite. My second principal became my friend and mentor, and even after many years, his policy with staff, his enthusiasm for his work and his forbearance to the activities of his employees were inculcated in his demeanor to us all. We had offices on the top floor of an exceedingly tall block and he arrived one day to find members of staff poised outside the door, on the basis that the keys were lost and we could not enter. He looked out of the corridor window, and observing that one of the office windows was open, decided against our remonstrations to climb through our window, crawl along a six inch wide ledge over a hundred feet from the ground, pressing against the wall until he reached the open window, lifting himself through, then opening the front door to us without taking a breath. He became an immediate hero, particularly as he was not young at the time, but what we would refer to as somewhat 'middle-aged'.

He has been instilled in my brain to this day; the various phrases that he imparted to me, which I carried with me throughout my career. One of his maxims was that to be a good

---

[*] Shopkeepers

18

accountant, time spent with a client was twenty-five minutes weather, and five minutes accountancy. The implication being, clients are to be respected and put at ease. Further, that one should be in practice when Income Tax is 5p in the £1.[*]

Thus clients would come to you not just for their taxation problems, but because you were good at what you did, thereby giving a lie to the general concept that accountants are solely in practice for the avoidance of taxation.

The general public was of the impression that we can tweak the tax laws and are the masters of avoidance, as opposed to evasion, which is illegal. He stated that the only instruments of value to an accountant were a pencil and rubber. You must remember, dear reader, that this was before the electronic gadgetry that is now available, but I suppose even these monstrosities have a delete button.

That was the good news. Now on to my first boss. He was young, but of Dickensian outlook towards his staff. He probably taught Mr. Scrooge. As an example, he invited the staff to his wedding, which of course we were reluctant to take up the offer as (a) it would have entailed us with our meagre salary to pay for some sort of present, (b) we could not decide the type of present appropriate to such a tyrant (although frightening suggestions were forthcoming), (c) we had enough of his company during our working time and did not wish to despair on a weekend. Further, so at the time my salary was the princely sum of 50p per week, I could not subscribe my share to anything other than a share of a daily newspaper. Nevertheless, we felt that if we did not attend, hell would be threatened the following Monday, so we accepted. The day came and we gathered in our small group at the corner of reception in the hotel. Reluctant and almost whimpering as a group, and upon his noticing us gathered there, he immediately came over and gave each of us a tray of canapés and

---

[*] English currency. 1 English pound = approx. $2.00

champagne to distribute amongst his guests. We realised upon observation that there was no staff as such, so we took over that role. Naturally as he had staff of his own, there was no necessity to employ others. It was a shame to the guests that various fingers were dipped into their drinks and in their food, but that was the least we could do and I understand that even in our restaurants this is not uncommon with obstreperous diners.

That was a minor side of his character, and there were many such instances of abusing staff – which is now an offence. In his eyes, the object in life was to have power over his subordinates. His policy with staff was that when we were out to see clients, we had to return to the office to 'clock-off', whatever the time. I had been sent to Aldgate in London to work and informed my employer that I was leaving to return to the office in Holborn. As I stepped off the bus nearest the office, a German V2 rocket (circa. 1944) landed nearby and I was thrown to the ground from the blast. The bus was severely damaged and pedestrians and passengers were left bleeding and dying. I was covered in dust and broken glass and there was mayhem. I hesitantly reached the office, dazed and bewildered in torn and filthy clothes. My esteemed boss, when I eventually reached the office, admonished me for being later than I stated and should not have arrived in such a condition. I tried to explain my predicament, which of course fell on deaf ears. As far as he was concerned, I was late and that was that.

My saviour – the managing clerk at the time – came to my rescue. He berated our boss, insisted that he open his beloved cocktail cabinet and give me a brandy to calm my nerves and for the shock. Naturally this was vehemently refused. My new friend kicked in the cabinet door, extracted the brandy, told me to drink and then suggested I go home – if that were possible – and not return for a few days. I left immediately and could hear both of them screaming at each other over such a blatant mutiny of the drink and the dismissal. My manager berated the boss on his heartlessness and the tyrant berated the clerk on interfering and minimising his authority.

When I returned to the office following that incident, my time with the company was limited and I eventually left under dire circumstances, with the threat that no references would be given. This I ignored and left to work with my saviour and mentor, mentioned before. Incidentally, my second employer was in partnership with another accountant, whose main interest was the bakeries that he owned and he was reluctant to attend the office, which of course put me off ever going into partnership. In that respect, I could not feel that I would work in conjunction with someone who had outside interests, or anyone that could work as sporadically as I did. Sometimes studying my naval at others working half into the night.

The above was a minor side of my first employer's character. I suppose his only saving grace, if there was one, was that he incorporated the name of his dog in the company and it became J Smith Fido and Company.

To start in practice in those far-off days, the only capital outlay that one would need was a desk, filing cabinet, two chairs and a telephone. The only fixtures and fittings were electric light, pen, pencil, rubber and typewriter. You were then in business. Naturally the only advertising the profession would allow was a nameplate to be attached prominently on the doorpost in the street outside your office. I did, at one time, take a chance and paint the office windows with my name and my profession, but of course, this was tastefully in gold leaf. The main ingredient for commencing trading was the acquisition of obtaining clients. You could not advertise, tout or (perish the thought), undercut other accountant's fees. You put up your sign and hoped that passing trade, recommendations, influence, friends and relatives, would pass through your office and eventually pay your fees and keep you above the bread line. In this respect my grandmother (of blessed memory) who knew a relation's accountant, summarised them all under the banner of 'bloodsucker' until I went into the profession. As she was very close to me, she then insisted I charge my prospective clients with as much, or more than I could get. Incidentally she was of foreign extraction and her command of the English language was minimal – to the extent of being non-existent. When I was with her and met her friends, she was so proud of me, and with her head held high would introduce me as 'an ac--t', which naturally embarrassed me no end not because of her unbounded pleasure in my achievement, but because at the time it seemed appropriate.

I mentioned that clients came by recommendations and relatives, and of course, if my father (rest his soul) had been a top sportsman, Ted Drake (Arsenal and England Soccer), Henry Cotton (Golf), Dennis Compton (Cricketer Middlesex and England), or even Fred Perry (Tennis) could have been clients. If he was in entertainment, I might have had Laurence Olivier, John Gielgud, or Ralph Richardson cross my portals. Unfortunately for me, but not necessary to him, he was a tailor. Interestingly, in the area where I lived there were many tailors and one in particular became a captain in the army during the war. As he was a humble worker, the conclusion everyone came to was that he must have been a member of a suicide squad and got promotion through wastage. He came back from the war and recommenced his trade. One day he put a card in a newsagents window requesting the services of a machinist, and they had to apply to 'captain so and so'. A tailor client of mine placed a card below requesting a machinist and to apply to 'corporal so and so'. As it was my father's trade, my first clients were naturally tailors and my first was named Merkin.

Later, when I employed staff, they requested that an additional member of staff should be a cat. Maybe because in my building they were ensconced in the basement and rodents might have joined our happy band. I, being an animal lover, and of course magnanimous to my staff agreed and when the kitten arrived there was a heated discussion as to naming it. They came to the conclusion that it should be called Merkin, who was not only one of my first clients, but the name for some reason seemed to amuse the staff. Thus it was NAMED. It was only when I matured enough that I found that in Hollywood a fake pubic hair for actresses was called a 'merkin', as such my pussy was appropriately named.

Of course to be a professional, it was incumbent upon all students to take the appropriate examinations of the controlling professional bodies. This entailed working during the day, and in most cases, studying through the night. One was expected to obtain advice and instruction from one's Principal – to be tied under Articles* for five years to either a decent, caring and considerate employer that would give up time to explain the intricacies of the profession, or to a tyrant, to prove to his clerk that he cannot impart any information on accountancy, as this was beneath him. This of course, shows the gamble that the young clerk takes for the next five years of his life.

To break Articles in the middle of the period was considered a heinous crime, and almost as difficult as requesting a salary. Your name could easily be banded about, and you could be ostracised among accountants as if you had the plague and three heads.

We as students, sitting for private examinations – for that is what the Institutes were – felt that at meetings of the council's bodies, they could control the entrants into the profession and stifle competition. We therefore devised a scenario whereby at a meeting of the council, the members would look at the list of accountants and decide how many new entrants there should be. They would then count out our examination papers and decide which ones were to be added to the list, regardless of whether we were successful in the examinations answers or not. As such, they could control the new entrants. Further, in

---

* Term for Accountancy Apprenticeship and contract

this connection they could take account of the elitism and snobbery of the so-called profession and only accept those that were, shall we say, of a certain class to keep up the pretence. In this respect, with my background, I would be way down the list if that were the case. My education being of the then council[*] school, and being the son of an artisan would push me lower than slime. Naturally this was speculation by us students, and in point of fact the results were consistent with what was expected from the honourable members and some passed because they had the knowledge and worked at it, while others of a more laid-back disposition probably failed.

I remember at a lecture given by one of the founders of at that time one of the world's leading accountancy firms, that when he was a student, he felt that *one question was going to be asked at his examination paper.*

He therefore learned the answer by heart and blow me down, the question appeared.

Since knowing the answer, he informed us that this snippet of information, throughout his professional career, earned the princely sum of 25 guineas[†] (£26.25). It proves that to prepare for the profession, the examination had no relevance. Incidentally, his favorite phrase was that accountants were the 'barnacles on the ship of industry' – quite apposite to current conditions.

Many large accountancy firms have management consultancy as an adjunct to their practice. This is all well and good for accumulating additional substantial fees, but do they know business? Are they working on the shop floor? Do they sit in the boardroom? Do they go out selling products? Do they make day-to-day decisions? By heck! They don't. Above all else

---

[*] Government State run school in England
[†] Old English term for a particular currency number

do they take? What I consider is an important ingredient in man/woman management, which is LOYALTY.

Many years ago, a client, who had a large furniture factory where frames were made, approached me. He wished me to commence, which in those days was called 'time and motion' study, on the factory and its workers. This was for me a great moneymaking scheme, with lots of time spent, statistics shown and reams of reports to concoct. I savored the moment, but in all honesty felt that a discussion with the client on the prospect in the first instance would be helpful, laying before him my observation prior to commencement of – in my opinion – this great confidence trick. I mentioned to him his first employee, whom he had known for many years and whom he could call upon for any emergency in the factory, at any time of the day or night, weekends included.

This gentleman would be at his beck-and-call regardless. I pointed out to my client that my perfunctory observation of the employee showed in his workstation he was not pulling his weight. I then suggested that my 'time and motion' study would throw up this situation and therefore 'QED'* – it would be advisable to dispense with his services. My client at once refuted this and pointed out that the chap in question was the most loyal person he knew. We therefore came to the conclusion that my report would have been disregarded, as such the whole exercise came to naught. I lost substantial prospective fees, but at least the loyalty factor prevailed, which pleased me morally, if not financially.

It's so easy nowadays to consider what the Americans unfortunately have coined the 'bottom line'; in other words, the profit motive. When companies are making a reasonable profit the immediate solution is to increase these profits by cutting overheads, and the most substantial and easiest are salaries

---

* Latin phrase; Quod Erat Demostrandum
Translated "it is proved"

and wages. This naturally creates redundancy and all that implies. The fact that the workforce is essential in a company, and the mainstay of production in manufacturing, does not seem to come into the equation, which means this method is the simple solution. Damn the fact that efficiency, new machinery, additional employee skills, sharper buying and better salespeople do not enter the frame. Apart from that, this does not seem to be the solution for the ills of the company as far as the consultants are concerned. It's an easier life, which of course increases their fees, and seems to be the best way of dealing with the problem.

Don't get me wrong, I have nothing against a company wishing to employ these 'experts'. I simply state that in most instances the solution rests with those in the boardroom who are familiar with the workings of the business, understand its intricacies, and hopefully between long lunches, constantly study their company's share price.

Have I an axe to grind? Too right I do, solely because during my professional career I have come across and have heard about mismanagement by directors, handling their company and consultants theories without practical foundation. In other words, monies wasted for no particular reason or return.

Now we come to the 'enemy', 'bloodsucker', 'silent partner', and/or thief – most of the adjectives that are applied by the public to the Inland Revenue* or Customs and Excise (VAT). As one famous politician stated, 'taxes and death are always with us'. He did not mention that even after death there are taxes in the form of Capital Transfer Tax, and we as accountants are employed as a buffer between 'them' and 'us'. They in their turn term us as 'Agents', which I suppose is true in the respect that we are not necessarily personally liable for any taxes due by our clients. However, we are subject to rules and

---

* Government Tax collection offices in England

are strictly forbidden to connive with the public to evade taxes. There are heavy penalties imposed upon us, even to the extent of a prison sentence, should that occur. Avoidance is legal; evasion is not. However, it was at one time implicitly understood by the Treasury that without our cooperation less taxes would be collected. I don't think that enters their head at the present time. They feel now that they are omnipotent and we accountants are treated no differently to other professions, and occasionally worse. One could in the past telephone the Inland Revenue and speak to an inspector on a personal or equal level.

Negotiating, or generally discussing, problems you might have personally, or for clients, would yield reasonably valued opinions and have them listen to your concerns. I found many to be quite human and occasionally with a sense of humour. Through protracted correspondence over a client's affairs, the inspector eventually wrote to me and in his letter stated 'we are skirmishing on the periphery', a wonderful phrase, which I have without his permission or paying him royalties. (I might add) I have used that phrase quite often when it applies. Some inspectors are intelligent, tenacious, understanding, negotiable, and down to earth. Others are high-handed, superior and bloody-minded, unlike common law where you are innocent until proven guilty. With the Inland Revenue, you have to justify all your claims and prove your figures. They don't necessarily have to prove anything. They could make accusations, and the most difficult argument I found was to prove a negative. They take malicious letters seriously and follow up every rumour or newspaper report. Any form of intelligence is pursued. If they thought you were paying insufficient Income Tax, one had to show them specifically the reasons why one felt that the tax laws were being adhered to. This could lead to a frustrating and eventually expensive time.

When it comes to eventual collection of Income Tax from those self-employed, this goes to the Collector of Taxes, which

27

is well named. They are the 'heavies', 'foot in the door' types who will not negotiate time frames for payment. As Income Tax for the self-employed was payable after money had been earned, unlike PAYE[*], which is payable on salaries paid monthly or weekly. They could be in a situation whereby in the year of payment, income could have dropped considerably – as such, the funds are not available. In a heaven-sent world, provision should be made for this eventuality, but we live in the real world where few consider their eventual liabilities, such as Income Tax. The person who puts their Income Tax in the tin on top of the mantle shelf together with the rent, light and heat, rates and savings, as they used to do in black and white films of the 'working class', does not apply in the present world. The Collectors' answer is that arrangements should be made for this eventuality. Human frailties being as they are, this is not as it was. Monies earned are usually spent in the cost of living, which perpetually rises and most live on a fairly tight budget. Unfortunately, or fortunately, the employees of the Inland Revenue are on PAYE and therefore a fixed income and do not understand or appreciate those that exist on a sporadic income. This causes a certain friction on both sides, and without much leeway given, Bailiffs and Bankruptcy are threatened and fear generated. I appreciate that some taxpayers are obdurate and never intend to pay anything including Income Tax on due dates, but the majority are reasonable and wish to settle their liabilities.

VAT[†] is administered, collected, and inspected by officers of the Customs and Excise – the same officer you see at docks and airports and whose main remit is to deal with smugglers and drugs. They are a powerful arm of the government — as such I always dissuaded clients to trade from home. A VAT inspection can therefore bring other factors into the equation. You have say, a porcelain clock proudly displayed in your room,

---

[*] Direct taxation
[†] Form of English Sales Tax 'Value Added Tax'

28

where the inspection is taking place. In the course of the visit the inspector may casually admire the clock, and you proudly say 'thank you' for the compliment. Further questioning by the inspector in a casual and friendly manner, enlists the information of its origin cost and country of purchase.

The fact that no duty or VAT had been paid could then become embarrassing, costly and freeze the atmosphere immediately. The inspector is still a customs officer, which is inbred and VAT is a necessary adjunct to his profession.

I had a client who had a manic, almost frightening hatred of VAT and their officers. It is probable that in the past his ancestors where either smugglers on the Cornish coast or pirates on the high seas. There was no other logical reason for this obsession. Nevertheless, he always charged the correct amounts and paid his liabilities on time. When a visit to his premises was arranged, he immediately went into action. First he would pick the darkest corner of his factory. He would then replace the electric bulb with one of twenty-five watts. A foot high desk would be placed with a stool of at least three feet for the use of the inspector – all purchased specifically for this purpose.

Next he would present his books of account. This was normal except that he numbered the pages of his records haphazardly. For example, it would commence with page '1' and the next page would be '12' and then '4', and follow with page '7' and so on. When they were presented to me for audit, he would give me an annotated, correct list. The inspector would show his frustrations throughout the visit. Some treated the whole matter with disdain and persevere, others would eventually have to give up and run screaming from the premises. My client treated the whole visit with unbounded glee, at the rustle of paper as the inspector flicked through the disorder presented to him. My client was always correct in his calculations and was never admonished or reprimanded, as his records were proved accurate, although in a mitigated mess.

Of course, it must be realised that the officers of the Inland Revenue and Customs and Excise are on average salaries and the psychology of their position must be difficult when they have to deal with captains of industry, sportsmen and entertainers, whose earnings are far in excess of theirs. Being British civil servants[*], their personal feelings cannot come into the equation. It has been rumoured, that for the officers to enquire into the affairs of the big earners would entail dealing with high powered lawyers and accountants and would conversely embroil the Government into vast expense to carry out their enquiries. Therefore, to investigate the small trader – who cannot afford such defiance – is easier to prosecute. This is probably unfair, but that is usually perceived as the norm.

When I first commenced practice, I took a one-room office above a hairdresser in London, which was on the cusp of the West End[†]. I began with a 'Mickawberish' attitude. Income £6.00, expenses £4.00 ecstasy! Income £4.00, expenses £6.00 misery! I was in the latter position, therefore I began a part-time insurance agency, used my office as an accommodation address, and tried consistently to negotiate a more reasonable rent with my landlord, on the basis that the smells from the hairdressing establishment and the fact that ladies were visiting my offices could be construed as being a property of ill-repute. All this was to no avail. However, my landlord – an ex-Indian Army Officer – threw me a lifeline. He suggested that if I would help him complete the coupon for the weekly football pools[‡], I would be entitled to a percentage of the winnings. All I had to do was enter the coupon with the numbers that he supplied, buy the postal order and submit them to the organisers. As he

---

[*] Paid by and/or work for the Government
[†] Nice part of central London
[‡] Soccer lottery

had a persuasive character and I was short of cash, I agreed to his request. I then began completing the coupons and sent them with the appropriate postal order, deducting all costs from the rent payable. However, my landlord, who was a severe alcoholic, disputed every time the rent was paid, as to the deductions I had made, and I eventually gave up the assignment and any thought of a winning percentage.

As I stated, he was usually in a drunken stupor, no doubt through his time spent in that continent. Some months later, he thought that he had won the first prize, which at that time was worth £75,000, a considerable sum in the 1950's. One had to pick eight noughts to represent football draws to win. That week there were nine draws and he had picked all nine. However, you could only have eight in a line and he had nine. This was done probably whilst he was drinking his gin. The coupon was invalid, and his claim rejected. He had won nothing. He began an immediate bender and after a short time was found dead. I suppose I did suffer a conscience, for if I had carried out his wishes, he might have been alive to collect his prize. I would have had the almighty problem of obtaining my commission, and would have probably have killed him myself, as he was obdurate and have refused. From then on, my luck went downhill rapidly. But c'est la vie. I knew from that experience any future monies I would receive would of necessity be from my professional work and not any extra curricular activities.

To an extent, very few accountants are what are commonly called business people. Not like in America, where even doctors and dentists are all in some form of business. I assume that our capitalist culture is different. It is a fact that accountants dealing with every aspect of business and getting a deep insight into the trading of most services or manufacturing companies would have an edge in thinking of obtaining an additional income and becoming the wealthy individuals they think they should be. But then we are considered staid non-gamblers, and without the risk-taking element. To an extent this is true. However, because we understand the pitfalls of business start-ups and a continuous trading environment, we become wary. We cannot – although we wish we could – 'fly by the seat of our pants' and take risks. We are not born entrepreneurs as others, and we understand that to make any business successful, your attention must be devoted to that cause, and one cannot play at being businesslike. We are not born that way. Our little grey cells can only accommodate the vagaries of our calling. We add up a personal balance sheet of advantages and disadvantages, inevitably being over-pessimistic. It is in our psyche. Oh to discard our inhibitions! To close our eyes, and take the plunge without a care, and start immediately with a factory, shop or service business. But this is not our *métier*. I will gamble on horses, lottery, sport, or at the casino, but naturally the result is almost instant. You win or lose immediately. In the commercial world this will take time and energy and there is the rub. I personally, always had a conscience over fee charging. What did my clients get? A nicely typed set of accounts in a beautifully prepared cover, which by its nature had to be out-of-date. What, in accountants speak, is of the 'historic convention'. A bit of correspondence, help with the Tax Return, some interviews and sorting out some box of invoices and torn account book. Then a bill is dropped in the post, which is expected to be paid within a reasonable time of receipt, i.e. by return. Deep down, what did I do for my exorbitant fee, which in other professions is laughable? I always felt that when professional fees were charged in the old guineas* e.g. £1.05p, that the 5p covered the overheads and the rest was profit. It was bizarre.

I still have nightmares over fee charging. Most of my colleagues considered my attitude to be on the verge of insanity. Their feelings were that they charged what they felt

---

* Form of old English currency

their clients could afford, and then some. This plus added overheads took the fee into the realms of Haley's Comet.

I well remember that the last practice I worked for had a minimum charge of 25 guineas (e.g. £26.25). I went to see a new client who was a small market trader in a deprived area of London. I mentioned the minimum fee – which I gauged to be a month's earnings for him – with trepidation, and secretly hoped that he would not join us. He looked at me aghast, stated that he knew no other accountants and reluctantly came to us. I must admit endeavouring to persuade him to try elsewhere, but he accepted our services.

I went away reluctantly, knowing full well he would struggle to pay our fee, which I was sure he would do come hell or high water. I think that incident set the foundation for my future charging fees. I felt then that having a hundred clients paying me £100.00 per year was preferable to one client paying me £10,000.00 each year. For if they left the practice the hole in finance would be enormous. Apart from that, they would be fickle and at one's beck-and-call continuously, whereas a client only paying £100.00 leaving is regrettable, but no appreciable loss of income. Not that I did not have some large fee paying clients, most of those having started with me in a small way and progressed to fairly large companies. However, fee charging is contentious. Undercutting is deeply frowned upon. Most London accountants, due to heavy overheads, usually charge the same hourly rate, even to the extent of minute charging. A client is expected now to pay for telephone, fax and ancillary costs as an addendum to the fee bill. This can cause havoc and has been known for firms to charge the time for preparing the bill to the client.

With the aid of computers, fees are now based on time spent plus expenses applicable to any client. This can therefore throw up anomalies. A persistent client can quite easily create a fee structure out of keeping with the work involved. Whereas a timid client with simple work involved can generate a nominal

33

fee, which to some accountants must be boosted to make it tolerable; therefore, fees can get out of hand and tip the balance. Accountants are now endeavoring to create a professional fee structure comparable to solicitors[*], and we all know the public's attitude towards that profession.

My practice was an eclectic mix of businesses and I was fortunate in that respect. It gave me an insight into business practice that I never would have obtained. This gave me a personal insight into the workings of a vast array of individuals and companies. Some accountants have been known to have an abundance of single business or professional types, such as taxi drivers, doctors, etc. I did not have that type of practice, for which I am eternally grateful. A varied practice is an interesting one, which was personally exciting to me, as this variation made each day open to a different problem to the previous ones. I had clients from most trades and professions. A client who working solely by gaslight, did the most intricate petit point for the antique trade to a large luxury car dealership. Each client had his own problems connected with his trade, but the ultimate aim was to see that the Government demands, albeit tax or VAT were adhered to. Regardless of the trade or profession, the end result was the same, and however large or small, our attitude to them has to be equal. A market trader or a captain of industry must be given the same courtesy, respect and comfort, and no favouritism shown because of the fee structure. It must be remembered that a problem, however large or small, is still personal.

A few of the cases that I have dealt with − out of many over the years − I have described in the following paragraphs, which I hope will be amusing, thought-provoking and help understand the profession from our side of the desk. Of course, the names of the clients have been changed to protect the guilty.

---

[*] Lawyers

34

Chapter 2

HAIRY MOMENTS

I am not against facial hair *per se*. In fact, at one time to look older, wiser and self assured, I grew a moustache. After many years, looking into the mirror, I realised that I was older, wiser and self-assured and got rid of the appendage. My son has had a moustache from the age of thirteen and still sports this hedge. I love him as ever, nevertheless.

I left my office one time, overburdened with a heavy workload – bedraggled and struggling to the car park, head bowed and fairly miserable. This was a regular occurrence. Not that I was that much overworked, just that I carried this heavy burden. It was because of my erratic form of working that I also had to take files home to work on them. During my traipse to collect the old banger[*] I was using at the time, I saw out of the corner of my eye an impressive character walking towards me. He was tall, wore a very expensive suite, an equally expensive coat – probably Vicuna – draped over his shoulders, covering his three-piece suit, which had a gold watch chain across the waistcoat, and to complete the ensemble a silver topped walking stick. The most outstanding item was a magnificent beard, reminiscent of the old 'John Player' cigarette packages

---

[*] Old car

of my youth. For those that can remember, it showed a sailor in a circle just head and shoulders with a magnificent black beard. It was of outstanding shape and style. The beard I saw was almost the same, but much curlier and blond, and tinged with a slight red colour, which matched the gentlemen's hair. This was also curly and beautifully coiffured, costing a fortune to be kept in the condition on show. He stopped before me, proud and imposing – a man of the world, self-assured and with supreme confidence oozing through his demeanor. To sum up, he was tremendous a figure! He stood before me with his magical blue eyes, looked down at me, and said in a deep cultured basso voice, "Hello Perry."

I looked up and stared at him and tried desperately to remember who he was. Passers-by were staring at him with a certain envy and not only from the men. Wondering how this odd couple should be facing each other, trying desperately to figure out why this magnificent specimen should bother with the likes of me. They probably thought I had accosted him for money and were ready to call the police.

He then said, "You don't remember me, do you? I'm Sherman."

Good Lord!!! At one time, at school, he was my best friend. I had not seen him for over twenty years. My mother was still friendly with his mother, and I had heard all about him from that source, that he was an extremely successful businessman, wealthy, charitable and a great son to his mother. He was overtly gay. In all the years that we were friends, I was ignorant of that fact. I knew that he was of above average intelligence, and when we were young we discussed our future work in life, and train driving and aeroplane flying was usually at the top of the list. However, when I asked him what he proposed to do, he informed me with an air of indifference that he wished to be an economist, which made me scurry home to look up this word in the dictionary. Such was the timbre of the man then, and it would seem that his brainpower had increased over the years and had not let him down.

In our youth I did not suspect his sexual proclivities, and as a young schoolboy I was unaware. What I understood from my mother was that he was now more gay than gay. He lived in a whopping great apartment with a Spanish manservant and had many friends of his own persuasion. His mother took pride in this situation and was more understanding than the general population of the time, and was quite open to my mother regarding the situation with her son. When I met him that day, this did not show. He was manly, everyone's idea of the perfect 'James Bond' – suave and sophisticated. The impression given was that women of all ages would worship at his feet. His beard therefore belied his natural desires. This nurtured my belief that a beard was probably a sign of untruth and of some insanity, which came to a head with my client, Tom Reynolds.

Tom was successful in business. He owned a factory, employing many staff engaged in welding. He was a deep-sea diver and combined underwater welding, which he near enough pioneered. He was a diver of immense ability, if a tad reckless, and was known amongst the diving fraternity as a great expert in cylinder, snorkel and full diving equipment. Tom was admired and respected in that community throughout the country and Europe and was favourably compared with the great divers of the past that pioneered the idea of underwater exploration to the masses. He also owned a private lake to experiment in and at one time invited me to participate in full diving gear. As I could not swim, suffered from claustrophobia and was an abject coward, I declined. However – and this is where the beard came in – for he was at that time supporting this growth. He became aggressive, which was not his nature, and insisted. His assistants began dressing me against all my protestations in a full rubber suit, and placed my feet in lead boots, but when it came to screwing the brass helmet on me, I screamed and almost went into a deep faint. Tom looked me straight in the eye and said that if he had not needed me as his accountant, he would have dumped me in the lake. His assistants cowered before his anger and began removing the gear, to my blessed relief. Tom, who was also dressed in diving gear, immediately had the helmet fixed to him, jumped into the lake and stayed down for two hours, whilst I cowered in the corner; the pump worked away, and I didn't utter a word throughout. On his return to the surface, he undressed reluctantly, beckoned to me to enter the Jaguar and drove back to his office in silence. He stormed into his office and slammed the door, and that was that!!! His secretary looked at me pityingly and suggested that I quietly fade away.

A few days later, his secretary rang me, "Guess what happened?"

I had no idea, apart from the fact that either the factory had burned down or that Tom had drowned himself, but by her tone something more serious had happened.

"Well," she said. "He arrived at the factory to find that the workers had gone on strike for the usual 'more pay and lesser hours'. They were standing outside the gates with various placards and chanting." This was more serious than I first thought. She carried on –

"They were quite abusive to the boss and he got into his car and came back after a time, took a placard out of the car and stood with his workers." Typical I thought …

"The shop steward approached him and said that he could not protest against his own factory. Mr. Reynolds haughtily informed him that as he was a member of the union, there was reason for him to protest and that he had as much right as a paid up member. It therefore became a farcical situation and naturally the strike petered out."

Tom then came on the telephone to me and said, "You know Perry, I'm so engaged in this diving I didn't realise their grievances and I shall probably agree to their demands."

I then asked, with a certain amount of trepidation, and with no apparent reason. "That's good news Tom, you still have it in you, and by the way where's the beard?"

"Are you a blithering idiot – why ask such a stupid question?" I muttered something incomprehensible.

"As you seem such a fool, I can tell you I haven't got one," he screamed down the telephone.

"Tom, I can't give an explanation for my asking you, I suppose I'm overworked."

That was always a great excuse for my blustering. However, my theory was reaching some sort of conclusion on facial hair.

A few months later he called me for a meeting. I was not obsessed and asked his secretary whether Tom was clean-shaven. She sounded sceptical and informed me that he was. I therefore attended the meeting with a certain joy, and found him amenable, intelligent and *au fait* with what was discussed. He was lucid and grasped the points under discussion immediately. Some momentous decisions were taken, followed by an excellent lunch, friendship and humour was the order of the day.

A few years later, he telephoned me late at night to give me the startling news that he had been arrested and remanded in custody, and requested that I visit him in prison as soon as possible. To say I was shocked was an understatement. He would give me no details over the telephone as to the charges and I arranged through the authorities to see him the next day. I arrived at the nineteenth-century prison, with an air of foreboding. The building was stark and uninviting. I pulled the chain bell, stated who I was and who I wanted to see, and was informed that I was expected and let in. I followed the warden with his massive chain of keys, who unlocked and then relocked the many iron gates that we went through with me following reluctantly behind. The prison showed its age with its bare stone walls and rivulets of water dripping down the walls. I was feeling more and more scared and depressed that I would never leave this Victorian monstrosity. How the prisoners and staff coped, I had no idea. To me this was hell on earth for all those in its precincts. Eventually, I was shown into a barred, dark room wherein sat my client on a wooden chair behind a tatty desk and a single, unshaded light bulb. He was sitting, bedraggled in a dirty pair of trousers and shirt, with a straggly beard and deep sunken eyes. I was shocked at his appearance.

"Tom, what happened?" I enquired, looking directly into his sunken eyes full of melancholy. He looked at me before answering.

"You won't believe this, " he began. "I came home from diving, and I think I had a small case of the 'bends'* and went straight to the bathroom, took my rubber suit off and went into the shower," he paused for a moment.

"When I came out there were no towels and I began calling down for some. When my wife arrived with them she became hysterical, saying I was unfaithful. Which to be truthful I was, as I was seeing another lady at the time." Tom hesitated and looked directly at me.

"Nevertheless, she began screaming and tried to hit me. I pushed her to the floor and grabbed the towel. She then went downstairs as I was drying myself." He hesitated again, and took a deep breath and continued.

"She must have then telephoned the police without me knowing and within a few minutes they arrived, found her sobbing and me flustered, as I was still in the nude. She then

---

* Lack of oxygen to the brain in diving

accused me of assaulting her but..." he paused again, and gave me that mournful look. I waited patiently for him to carry on, but then he began sobbing quietly. I had known him to be a strong individual and this was the last thing I expected. I waited for him to compose himself, giving him – I hoped – a sympathetic glance. He continued.

"I'm sorry, " he apologised and continued. "The worst part is that she accused me of raping my daughter, who as you know, is only fourteen. One policeman immediately took my arm and held it firmly and the other went upstairs with my wife to see my daughter. They found her on the bed crying and she told the policeman that I had gone into her bedroom, naked and attacked her. Without further ado, they arrested me and locked me into their car and went back to the house to take statements."

"Were you still in the nude?" I asked.

"Apart from the towel I was," he looked blank at that moment. "Oh yes, they gave me a blanket from the house, for decency I suppose. They then took me to the station, charged me for rape and assault and locked me into a cell." He began shivering, drank some water and said, "I was informed that a senior officer would call on my wife, together with a policewoman to take more formal statements and that the outcome would be that I would be remanded in custody and taken before the magistrates the next morning. They did promise to bring me some clothes from home and allow me to ring my solicitor."[*]

He began sobbing again and I waited quietly for him to continue.

"Their statements were devastating, as they repeated the assault and rape and had signed the statements." I looked at him and felt this was too much to take in. He said, "Well, they

---

[*] Lawyer

41

stuck to their stories, which I vehemently denied. I was then remanded to this god forsaken hellhole for my next committal hearing." This was devastating news and I felt that at this stage, I would not add to his mental and physical problems, but be sympathetic and not pursue any further questioning.

"So Tom, what do you want me to do, anything that you require or need?" I asked. He looked at me carefully and said.

"I've got to keep the business going. They don't know the situation at the factory and my solicitor has told my secretary to tell them I have gone diving abroad, and do not know when I'll be back." He looked pleadingly at me.

"They must not know, and I implore you to keep this quiet. They have enough orders to keep them working for sometime and all I really want from you is to keep the business floating. I have arranged with my bank for you to sign cheques and just keep an eye on the business, visiting when you can just to assure them that I will be back as quickly as I can." For the first time in our meeting he smiled.

"They know me – my absence at the moment won't cause any problems, for you know I do take off occasionally and during those times I'm incommunicado."

His pleading, and situation, made up my mind immediately.

"Of course, Tom, I will deal with this as best as I can." I also added. "Whatever you have done in the past – and Tom you have done some diabolical things as you know – I'm with you a hundred percent and must add that this accusation is unbelievable and of course, I accept you're innocent". He got up from his chair and came towards me. The warden in the background told him to sit down. I put my hand out to him and shook his hand, which I found clammy, matching the beads of perspiration on his brow.

I left just after saying, "I'm sure that this is a pack of lies, and knowing your daughter she was probably influenced by your wife. My feelings are that after finding out about your girlfriend, she wanted to hurt you as much as she was hurt, but damn it all, why involve your daughter? That apart, you can rely on me with the business and if you have an opportunity to contact me at any time please do so." I left him sitting forlornly by the desk, with his head in his hands. I had never ever seen him so dejected. He was then tapped on the shoulder by the guard and he followed him out of the room, shuffling along beside him, head down and his straggly beard looking as forlorn as its owner.

Leaving the prison was as difficult as entering. To me it was a salutary lesson, and although there have been reforms in the system, I still cannot watch films or television programs that deal with this aspect of life. Some months later, I had kept in communication with his office, and visited regularly, although no one, had heard from Tom; things seemed to be working smoothly within the business and any hitches were resolved by a combination of his secretary, salesman, foreman, and in some small measure, myself. I decided one day to attend the company, as my usual visit, to be greeted by the staff, cheerful and smiling. The foreman gave me a grin and a thumbs-up. Everyone on the factory floor was labouring away with added zest and there seemed to be an aura of goodwill in the factory. I climbed the stairs to the offices, and the secretary had a smile on her face as wide as the Amazon. Her greeting to me was chatty, which was unusual in such a severe lady. I immediately became suspicious, and naturally the first thing a man does in such situations is check his flies!* This I did and was comfortable with the result. I was even offered coffee and biscuits. This made me doubly suspicious, as I usually had to scrimmage around for these delicacies. To this lady, any morsel

---

* Trouser zip

of food or drink during working hours was an anathema to her, as work came first and frivolities were kept outside work.

I looked at her closely and asked, "Everything alright?"

She lowered her eyes, which made her quite demure and said, "Yes, Mr. St. John. As the spare office is being used at the moment, why not do your work in Mr. Reynolds office?" This in itself was unusual, as I had been allotted an office. My temporary office was normally used for storage of documents and therefore slightly cramped. Mr. Reynolds office was usually reserved for himself and occasionally for meetings with staff and discussions. I opened the door, and there was Tom! Well-dressed, shaven, with an enormous grin. Naturally I stepped back in amazement.

"Tom?" I queried, which of course was silly.

"Hello, Perry," he said casually, as if the past months had not occurred. I waited expectantly for any explanations from this man he had transformed himself into, from the broken prisoner I had met, to this suave and self-assured individual shaking my hand.

"Sit down," he said with a smile. "And drink your coffee, later we'll have something stronger over lunch."

How normal! I wanted an immediate explanation, but thought it best to bide my time.

"I see you're surprised. No wonder. You still expected me to still be in the nick."* I nodded and automatically sipped my coffee and munched a biscuit.

"Well, I would have been in that abominable place still if an arrangement with the cow had not been made." He continued.

---

* Slang for prison

44

"An arrangement! What arrangement?" I queried. Tom smiled again, very happy with himself.

"The arrangement, if you could call it that," he said. "That my wife Valerie forced me to firstly give her a divorce. Which in a way I was hankering after, as Perry, frankly it was no great shakes. The second was that I gave her the house and twenty thousand pounds," he winced slightly. "That part hurt. Nevertheless, I agreed as I wanted to get back to work and my current lady friend was pressing me to marry her, which of course I will do as she stood by me during the ordeal and accepts my flights of fancy with regard to the diving."

"But Tom," I said. "That's blackmail."

"I know that only too well, but at least it got me out of that god-forsaken hole and back to some normality." He was serious for a moment. "Incidentally, they found out that my daughter was untouched and unfortunately concocted the story under the influence of Valerie – poor kid."

At that moment a flash of despair crossed his face.

"I did try to speak to her and tell her that she was not to blame and I still loved her and held no grievance. Whatever she needed in the future I would be there whatever."

He looked down at this point, the dejection showing on his face again.

"The one saving grace in all this sordid business is that Valerie has been charged with wasting police time. Nevertheless I still would not want to see her going to prison. I've already gone through that and wouldn't wish the experience on anyone, even Valerie."

He then brightened up and said, "I can tell you, Perry, that when the divorce is through, I'm going to marry Joan, my girlfriend, and still hope that my relationship with my daughter can be normalized." He then became business-like, rustled papers on his desk, picked up the telephone to his secretary and asked her to bring in the current reports on the company. I looked up at him and watched the past few months slip away to oblivion. There was this man, the antithesis of that person I saw those months ago, sitting dejected and in abject misery in that bleak and revolting prison – a period in Tom's life, which he had blotted out completely and was not the boss, the gaffer, the governor that all his staff admired. He thanked me for the work I had done and said that whatever my account was to look after the company, he would happily pay, which he did within the month that it was submitted.

I did not realise at the time, that my helping him with the business was good grounding for what was to follow a year later. It was then that Tom telephoned me to inform me that he was going to marry Joan that coming Saturday. A registry office and no guests, witnesses if possible would be dragged from the street. Would I again run the business for the two weeks he was on vacation for his honeymoon? Of course, I acquiesced, although it was a drag to keep on going seventy-five miles each way to his office.

I said to him, "Tom, if anything urgent crops up, how do I contact you? Where are you going?"

"That's for you to find out," was his answer.

"Tom, at least last time I ran the business I unfortunately knew where you were," I replied.

"Look, Perry, this is my honeymoon. I want to forget the past and apart from that, what could possibly go wrong that you have to contact me?" He was sounding somewhat belligerent.

"Well you're probably going abroad, which was different to last time. By the way how's the beard?" I don't know why I asked that stupid question. A rush of blood to the head I suppose. He answered.

"Yes, I'm going abroad and you don't have to know where. And of course I have a beard. Why ask such a stupid question?" I stammered something incoherent and wished him well. I wasn't invited to the wedding. Why should I? I mean I only stuck by him through his travails! I helped in some small measure to carry the company and was expected to in the future. I was not a friend, and doing what I did I got a reasonable fee, which always helped as I was in my usual parlous state. However, he did pile responsibility on me without a 'by your leave', and I thought that at least we had built up some form of friendship. But you realise after a time that friendship with clients is a rare commodity. You are only as good as your last set of accounts. Apart from that, I tried not to have intimate relationships with clients of the friendship kind, although sometimes this was offered to the extent of purchasing things much more cheaply – but then the friendship and client could come to grief if the product purchased on the cheap was found to be faulty. The old maxim of never mixing business with pleasure still applied. When Tom at that time informed me that he had facial hair, a feeling of foreboding encompassed me and I knew that no good could come from this trip and my running the company smoothly. My prejudice came to the fore. I was being paranoid.

Good Lord! It was only for two weeks for Christ's sake! What could go wrong? The devil at my back laughed hysterically and said wait. He was not wrong. The problems I encountered were far above the norm. Even if during that time the factory had blown up and all had perished, it was nothing to what I encountered in my own mind – far more dramatic. The beard, not knowing where Tom was, coupled with the fact that I had to make that commuter journey a few times a week was definitely not to my liking. My only salvation, it would seem, was to keep fingers crossed and pray to all religious gods for safety and guidance during those fateful two weeks.

Immediately on the Monday following the wedding, I was sitting as usual in my office, surrounded by masses of paperwork, which I did not fancy tackling. I looked out of the window, then studied my navel (which I was prone to do quite often). I must have been suffering from a deep sense of extra sensory perception. I was short with my staff that morning and had an unpleasant weekend, solely because of my brooding. I knew in my heart it was going to be a 'black day'. I knew immediately when my secretary phoned me to inform me that Tom's company was calling and it was urgent. I knew and my thoughts and feelings were reaching a zenith! This was it!! Doom! Doom!

"Put them through," I said, in a hysterical voice. Tom's secretary came on the telephone. I could tell at once there was panic in her voice.

"Mr. St. John?" The telephone shook in my hands and I could tell that the same thing was happening to her.

"We have a severe problem here." I immediately imagined that the factory had indeed blown up, but then common sense prevailed and I realised that she was on the telephone to me. What a logical brain I possessed. Of course she could have telephoned from outside. Nope, that would have entailed hearing 'pips'[*] from an outside telephone. When she had first spoken to my secretary I would not hear them. OK, so I was wrong! Do something to me for that lack of logic.

I tentatively enquired from her, "what?"

"Well, I think you know that we have four men on a listing ship in the North Sea, welding plates where it was holed and trying to take the ship to Holland for full repairs." This was ridiculous, as I had no knowledge of this particular incident. Tom was not always forthcoming in his instructions to me when I had to look after the company. Such workings were normal to

---

[*] Telephone tone from public call box

48

him, but too incidental to impart to me. He felt that it was unnecessary to impart technical information to a layman like myself. I did know that in the past the company had taken on unusual work and the salvage of small vessels were occasionally taken on.

"So!" I enquired as casually I could muster.

"Well," she said – "They have telephoned me by ship-to-shore radio and said that they want an immediate rise in pay, otherwise they are arranging to abandon the ship." This was below the solar-plexus remark.

"They can't do that," I exploded. "If they abandon the ship, it will be a hazard to other shipping in the area."

"I know that," she said huffily. "But they have insisted that they talk to someone of authority, and who better than you, Mr. St. John," she responded – her voice taking on a smarmy tone. Got you, was implied!

"You can't deal with it then?" I implored, knowing full well that she would not and could not deal with it and take on a responsibility that she could happily place at my door.

"No Mr. St. John," she was emphatic. Then her tone changed slightly. "I tell you what I will do, and that is contact them and tell them that you are in charge and it would be best to speak to you."

She then replaced the telephone. She was now immediately taken off my Christmas list, and any other list I held for whatever purpose. I sat there, doomed. What could I negotiate with? I knew nothing of the work they were doing and not even the amount of salaries they were drawing. It was a dilemma for which I was not prepared. Thank you, miss! In all the time I had dealt with Tom and my visits I was not ever informed of his secretary's name. As in all his dealings she was just 'her' – you can ask 'her' for anything. Coffee, files, papers, and correspondence, it was always 'Oh, just ask her'.

At this stage, 'her' seemed appropriate. I did not want to start asking her name as this might have 'rocked the ship' (oh, what an unfortunate phrase at that time). What to do? What to do? My brain was in turmoil. I had nothing to work on. My secretary rang me to say that there was a call for me from some distant crackly phone that she could hardly hear. This was it. Crunch time! Then this distant voice came on.

"Mr. St. John?" this disembodied voice enquired.

I reluctantly said, "Yes."

"Well you know we are on this ship in the North Sea and we want more money otherwise we leave," he sounded aggressive. This was no good.

"You can't do that," I retorted, trying to sound officious. I further endeavored without success to imply that I was angry. "And without Tom's permission I can't agree to your request." This was stalling, I know, but I tried. Then this disembodied voice gave me the *coup de Grasse*.

"We want you to visit the ship and talk, otherwise we abandon."

"What, how can you do that?" Feeling slightly faint.

"That's up to you."

"Don't do anything rash until I contact you again," I shouted with fear. The voice came back –

"Don't make it too long before you call," and with that the telephone went dead. I had to think quickly, which in my present state seemed a Herculean task. There was, as far as I was concerned, very few options open to me. The first was to inform the Coastguard. The second, which was equally important, contact my client. At this time the Coastguard seemed to be favourite to tackle the problem and try to convince the mutineers of their criminal ways. So I telephoned them and explained the situation. They took the problem in their stride. As

I expected, they were efficient and calm. The gentleman to whom I spoke accepted the problem without qualm. He said he would speak to the ship, lay down the law, and if I wished, they would have a helicopter available for me to visit the crew.

This news imparted the fear of death. The ship was listing at a roughly forty-five degrees, in a heaving sea. I hated flying, did not wish to be taken by helicopter to a ship miles from anywhere, and to be lowered by, I suppose is called a breeches buoy, did definitely not appeal. Further, I was a cowardly custard – fearful of my own shadow, and even at that time slept, as I still do, with a teddy bear. I was a whimpering, frightened individual at the best of times. The prospect of the future adventure almost gave me the 'vapours'.[*] I thanked them profusely and said I would wait for their call to the ship, and put on a brave face and thank them for the helicopter ride, which I looked forward to with unbounded pleasure, but hoped that it would not be necessary, liar that I am!

The chief Coastguard telephoned me a short time later and said, "I have spoken to the ship and the crew are adamant. I pointed out to them that they are committing a criminal offence by abandoning the ship, which they acknowledged that you had already informed them of that fact. Nevertheless, they still feel that a visit from you would resolve the situation and would save us the problem of sending a ship to them to tow them in, which of course would take time. We could of course issue an arrest warrant in Holland when they arrived, but this would take legal problems and if it could be resolved by your visit, all the better. I shall therefore have a helicopter standing by at Manston[†] if you wish. Just let us know," and with that the telephone went dead.

I was perplexed. At least the Coastguard was willing to cooperate. There were small mercies about, but it was a big 'but' how I was to resolve the situation. Think! Think hard Perry.

---

[*] Feeling faint
[†] Airfield in Kent

I must not add to my fears. Inspired thought processes had to come to the fore. I paced the office trying to think of a solution. The easiest of course, would be to accede to their demands. This however, went too far. For if I did, within a few days further demands would be forthcoming, and if I agreed to be frank to ease my fears, by the time Tom got back their salaries would be through the roof and my reputation would go the other way.

I had been told by the Coastguard that they could not land the helicopter on the ship and I would be lowered by cable. I was also informed that my only requirement was to have a head for heights. Head for heights? I could not stand on a stool without feeling queasy. Imagining that I would require wires coming down from the ceiling, to which I could hold to steady myself if I was more than a foot above the floor. Plan 'B' was my only option. It eventually struck me that Tom's favourite resort was Majorca. I plumped for that and telephoned the Foreign Office to obtain the Consul's number on that island. I eventually got through to this well-spoken, slightly supercilious individual and explained the situation. He seemed, by the tone of his voice, incredulous and thought this was a wind-up, and if not a wild goose chase, would spoil his day on the beach. However, knowing the seriousness of the situation of the ship and that the Coastguard had been informed, he stated that his minions would comb the area hotels and see what he could come up with. But no promises were given. Typical civil servants speak, but I had no alternative. This was the last throw. I was, I knew, clutching at straws. Time was not on my side. I informed the men on the ship that I was reluctantly prepared to visit them, but in the meantime they should not do anything stupid, and wait for further instructions. Their spokesman became more aggressive and belligerent at my tone, but nevertheless agreed to wait a little longer for a solution.

I cancelled all my calls for that day, except from the ship or Consul. I paced the office, chain-smoked, drank innumerable cups of coffee and gave serious thought to my will. My mind was in turmoil and I knew that I was clutching at straws with the Consul finding Tom. I reviewed my run of luck over the previous years and found that it was seriously lacking in that department. Would I find Tom? Was the vessel being abandoned? Was I going to be helicoptered and lowered on a listing ship? Was I going mad? Was I relying too much on the supercilious Consul? Was I correct in my assumption that Tom was on the island? Was this a situation that I was trained for? The latter question was emphatically NO! Instinct, flash of genius, extra-sensory perception, or sheer luck could be the answer and save my reputation and neck.

Time stood heavy. My secretary rang me to inform me that the ship was on the telephone again. I tried to play for time and told her to tell them I was preparing to go to Manston, when I had heard further from the Coastguard to catch the helicopter, and if it was missed, like the buses another one was following. I was informed that a dead line time was being discussed and could not, and would not be changed. Blackmail was my first thought, but I had to do something – darkness was not far off. I had only a short while before I had to take that horrendous ride in the dark by searchlight, and at night the sea could be choppier than it is in daylight. I was even tempted to ring the metrological office for an assessment of the weather, but if that was bad, I would either just die or to put myself voluntarily into a mental hospital, happy in the knowledge that I would not have to face this situation. With my heart pounding I was pleased enough to contemplate that a heart attack was on its way and I was going to embrace this with grateful thanks.

I informed the Coastguard of the latest developments and they assured me that whilst the ship was manned and still afloat they would await my instructions and the helicopter would stay on stand by – and incidentally they were quite happy with the situation as costs for their service were still rising. This was a new development, as I believed, wrongly of course, that as this was a hazard to shipping and as a part of their job there would

53

be no charges incurred – another balls-up that I had made in my calculations – and another cross for me to bear and to explain eventually to my client. I now realised to keep staff and a helicopter on stand-by was a horrendously costly business.

It was then I heard from the Consul. When my secretary informed me that he was on the phone, I immediately dropped to my knees, shaking and moving my head backwards and forwards, and my eyes rolling to the ceiling.

I tentatively answered the telephone and the Consul said, "I have found Mr. Reynolds," and that Tom would be telephoning me later. Oh what a relief! All my instincts were correct. I could have hugged the Consul, his staff, his wife, his mother, his children, the cleaning lady, security guard and all who serve Her Britannic Majesty's interests throughout the world.

Then Tom rang.

"How did you find me? Why did you find me? And what the bloody hell are you playing at disturbing my honeymoon." Irritability could be ascertained, and a little anger in his tone. Further, the loss of a reasonable client in acquaintanceship and fees were immediately envisaged.

I explained the situation to him about the welder's demands and the predicament that this caused me. I laid it on thick. I emphasised the arrangements that I had put into place with the Coastguard and that I was prepared to visit the ship with their help. He started laughing.

"You bloody fool! I'm going to make a fortune from the salvage. Give the buggers what they want and insist that the ship docks in Holland A.S.A.P." With that he put the telephone down. I telephoned the mutineers and negotiated a fee with them, to which they seemed satisfied. Furthermore, (and this is where I put on my strongest voice), I do not wish to hear any further nonsense from them. They acquiesced and promised that the ship would dock as requested. I then spoke to the Coastguard informing them that I would not require their admirable service and the helicopter could be cancelled and put to more humane use. A bill was forthcoming from them in due course. I then collapsed in a heap on the floor. I still occasionally dream of being winched onto a ship in a raging storm and being blown by the howling wind hither and dither, dangling above the ocean on a rope, being soaked to the skin and waking up to find that my hot water bottle has sprung a leak.

Chapter 3

FEET OF CLAY

My cousin telephoned my office one day. I had not spoken to him for some years. He was the renegade of our small family. It was believed that he was running some nefarious businesses, but in fact, he owned a private members club in Soho[*]. In that period it was well known, and in the 1960's was a centre for those in the entertainment, newspaper, and advertising businesses. It was quite up-market for the time, where drinking and literate conversations were the norm. It was that my cousin owned a West End club, which my family did not accept. To me, his work was glamourous and interesting and he led a life that I deeply craved. But I was staid, and basically a daydreamer – a veritable 'Walter Mitty'. My mind was and is, mixed with thoughts of heroism and derring-do. There was adventure coupled with a need for adult and well-informed conversation. I wished for a meeting of minds, wherein I could hold the floor with erudite talk – a minefield of emotions that I controlled with the practicalities of my profession, and that showed I was a staid individual. But still my cousin spoke to me as if I had recently conversed over general mundane topics without the

---

[*] Entertainment section of London

intervening years being discussed. We naturally talked about the family, without a comment from him, except to say that he was still the outcast and felt that he could not make amends. He also wished to see me professionally as he was thinking of going into partnership with a film producer of his acquaintance. Then he mentioned the chap's name, Jack Walker. I hesitated for a moment and asked him to repeat the name, which he did and we then went onto talk on generalities and made an appointment for discussions in week's time.

As I replaced the telephone, various emotions came over me. The years dropped away in an instance. Jack Walker! I could not believe it. Not because he was a film producer, for I had not heard about him from that source, but because when I was in my very early teens, I belonged to a boys' club. I was interested in all its activities – chess, drama, but particularly in cricket. This was my game. Not of course, that I was that good. Surprising enough, that was the only game my family seemed to have taken to their heart. My uncle was a professional and groundsman[*]. One cousin did captain an army battalion. My father was avidly interested in the game and his mother, my grandmother – her being of foreign extraction – enjoyed the cricket teas when her son was playing. I believe if she did not understand anything truly British, she did know the LBW[†] rule. That was something to be proud of. No umpire was safe when she was around. Shouting obscenities in a strange language put them to flight. When she did not agree with their decision.

Further, my mother when she lived alone faced a famous cricket ground from her apartment and would spend time on her balcony, watching and commenting on the play to her neighbours. So you see, cricket was part of my life and this is where Jack Walker came into the picture. He was a member of

---

[*] Term for those revered personnel who take care of the field of play in cricket

[†] LBW is a form of an 'out' in cricket 'Leg Before Wicket'

the same boys' club and extremely popular. However, his main claim to fame was that he was captain of the cricket team and its star player. He played the game with what I can only describe as panache and beauty. He batted like a dream. He was tall and, a magnificent stroke player of unbounded skill. Admired and respected by our opponents and worshiped by his team, he was a schoolboy champion – the boy wonder on the cricket pitch. To me, a young boy, he was my hero.

He was a few years older than me, and naturally taller with blond flowing hair and an air of elegance in his dress code and game. Admiration from me was an insufficient description of my feelings at the time. I would, if pressed, lay my life down for him. Don't think that it was a schoolboy crush, it was solely hero-worship. I cleaned his cricket bat voluntarily. I followed him on the practice field and attended all his matches, and cheered to the rooftops when he batted and scored runs. Even if he did not score, I was still enamoured.

The day he would choose me for the team, I became excited, flustered and could not sleep. I was 'walking on air', in 'seventh heaven' and tongue-tied. I practiced, and boy did I practice! On a match day, after carrying his cricket gear, I just stood open mouthed, and to share the batting with him was the pinnacle of my life. After the game, I endeavored to speak to him but it was impossible for the words to come out. I stammered and spoke supreme gibberish. I just followed him wherever he went, puppy-like. I'm sure he realised something was going on, but he seemed to take my devotion as a matter of course. When he praised me for something I had done, which I must admit was not often, it was as if the heavens had opened and choirs were singing. I know that this sounds terribly dramatic and maybe smacks of something more sinister than it actually was. Nevertheless, in my innocence, I was smitten and devoted. Not sexually, I must add. That did not enter my young head, it was just a teenage thing similar to young girls and pop stars I suppose. Admiration, devotion and unlimited pleasure in being with him as a supreme sportsman, whom I hoped to emulate, but which never came to fruition.

Later on in our relationship, we both went our separate ways and our paths did not cross for many years. There was no word of him or rumours he just disappeared. Of course, I studied the sports pages of newspapers to see if his name was ever mentioned in county cricket, or even hopefully playing for England, until that call from my cousin. All the emotions that I had came flooding back to me from hearing that name. I was a schoolboy again! I tried desperately to banish these feelings. I endeavoured to recapture my maturity prior to the telephone call, to no avail – I reckon that the week prior to the meeting was the worst time of my life. My professional career during that time was in shatters – I was a blithering idiot, incoherent and forgetful. Life was on a down slope. I was excited and apprehensive for the meeting. My staff and family could not understand my predicament, the constant flushes and perspiration, my non-understanding of simple tasks and preponderance to look blankly when others were looking at me or seeking advice. I contemplated taking time off from work until the appointed time, but then my professional upbringing kept on coming up with practical solutions to my predicament, which of course I ignored. I was me, a younger teenager in mind. I was bewildered with the forthcoming prospect of meeting my hero again, this tall handsome elegant mature guy. The one who played dream cricket, an angel of the willow*, a colossus on the pitch, of infinite wisdom on the game, and a martyr to my thoughts and emotions.

The day before that fatal day was a complete haze. Only my natural instinct and inbred homing device enabled me to go to the office. I did not remember waking up, dressing and reaching work. Food and drink, of course, did not pass my lips, for if it had, it would not have stayed long within me.

---

* Cricket Bats can be made of wood from a Willow Tree

This was where a certain inner logic took over. I knew I was going to be sick, and I was within an hour of the meeting. Why had I arranged the conference for the afternoon? Common sense now dictates that it should have been at 5 a.m. or even earlier, to save my heartache and well-being, to ease my trauma, to save me at the time and peace of mind and emotions gathering in my body, to calm me and make me normal again. I barked and rasped. I paced and sat; I picked up the phone to my secretary, asking time and time again whether my clients had arrived. She became short with my continuous demands and I think she thought that I was demented and felt a touch of sympathy might not go amiss. I could not tolerate it, and told her so in no uncertain terms. She entered my office endeavouring to calm the situation, although not knowing the reason for my stupid behaviour. Of course, she did not know, neither did family or staff know the turmoil I was going through. I told her bluntly only to disturb me when they had arrived and sent her away with a flea in her ear. I think she cried quietly outside my office. Sympathy is all very well at the appropriate time, but this was not it. If this situation would happen now, counsellors would be summoned, but in those far off days grit and stiff upper lips were the norm. It was expected that one did not collapse under emotional strain. Forget all; shoulders to the wheel. Life must go on, and signs of feelings must be curbed at all costs. Growing up was the answer to all ills, whether it be in mind or body. Act like a man – which in my mind was solely to leave the toilet seat up. It was the epitome of being of the species, defiance in the face of those around you, especially the ladies. How all this applies to baby boys I'm still trying to figure out. With regard to the ladies, crying and tantrums were their prerogative. A firm but fair demeanour was that expected of the British male. It was said, that for men, life could be a gas if one's demeanour could not be bent. The allotted time for the meeting passed and there was no sign of my clients. I was demented! Delirious! Shaking! Insane!

After ten minutes, I opened the window of my office and contemplated throwing myself through it. Death would be a pleasant relief and my salvation. Then I realised that my office was on the ground floor. Throwing myself through would only hurt my pride and probably break my ankle. I searched the room for signs of poison that I could take to relieve my soul. Nothing. There was no rope in the office for hanging from the lights in the ceiling, apart from the fact that they were hidden in the false ceiling. I suppose I could have strangled myself with my bare hands to relieve the pressure, but thought better of it. Is there no hope or means for a suicidal maniac to get rid of himself? Why aren't the means available when they are required in such dire circumstance? How unfair!

Then my secretary informed me my clients had arrived. I apprehensively told her to tell them to come to my room. Without knocking, the door opened, not by my cousin but by Walker, who barged in and sat in the chair in front of my desk. My cousin followed behind. We exchanged pleasantries. My mind however, was not on the meeting and I answered perfunctorily and on autopilot, all the time staring at Walker. From what I could tell, he was roughly my size in height, but not in build. He was gross! And I mean gross! His head was bald, apart from a wreath of hair. His face florid, and a Churchillian[*] size cigar was firmly clamped to his sagging mouth. I stared at this monstrosity of a human being, trying desperately not to recognise any features in his face from the past.

Unfortunately, there was a semblance of recognition. I did not want to believe it or accept it. He asked me if he could call me 'Perry' and I wanted to reply emphatically no. Even 'Sir' from this monstrosity would not be acceptable, but I did not reply.

---

[*] Former Prime Minister of England, Winston Churchill famous for his cigar smoking

Discussions began concerning the partnership, but my heart and mind were not with it. I was 'flying by the seat of my pants' throughout. Still staring at this ogre, which he in his ignorance, he ignored, I must say that the terms mentioned and the talks were in full favour of my cousin, which surprised me, and I became suspicious, but deep down I did not wish him to go into the business with this egomaniac. When the discussions were ending, I could not contain myself any longer. I suddenly blurted out and asked whether he had ever been a member of our boys' club. Hoping for a negative reply, he gave me a quizzical look, and said that he had. I plunged in, with abject hesitancy, and asked him about cricket. His reply was devastating. He was emphatic that he hated the game. That did it! I was ready to commit murder. I searched my desk for a weapon. I contemplated pencils, but their points would break. I then saw what I was looking at. It was a letter opener, made of steel and felt solid in my hand. I grabbed the handle with relief and white knuckles. Anatomically I thought I could gauge roughly where his heart was amongst the flab. I felt that I could lunge over my desk, force the paper knife roughly through the chest with a twisting motion. I did not care whether blood would spurt all over my cousin or me. Death, I hoped would be instantaneous, and revenge sweet. The deed would be done, and knowing that our judges at the Old Bailey[*] are fair-minded, particularly over cricket. I would probably be kindly admonished, released immediately and obtain sympathy and maybe a place in the Hall of Fame at Lords Cricket Ground.

Unfortunately, my staid mind came into play and I did nothing to my enduring shame. I stared at Walker with hate, which of course he did not notice. Eventually my cousin noticed my demeanour and said that my eyes seemed glazed, and my face white, and enquired whether I was well. I blurted out that I was somewhat overworked, did not have breakfast or lunch and

---

[*] Famous English Court Building in London

felt slightly dizzy. He naturally was sympathetic. Walker did not say a word, but continued to smoke that abominable cigar, causing fog in the office, which became almost impenetrable. He seemed to sneer at my weakness and gave the impression that he could not be bothered with this weakling before him. He got up to leave and asked me, surprisingly enough, what my fee for the interview would be, pulling out of his pocket a wad of notes. I was tempted to request the lot and then some, but my conscience got the better of me and I mentioned a figure. He peeled off the notes and threw them on the table, and walked out. My cousin thanked me, wished me better and stated he would be in touch.

The deal we discussed, from what I could remember at the time, was especially good for my cousin, but I felt like that if he continued with Walker (the Beast), it would all end in tears. All right, I was biased through my emotions. Nevertheless, I tried to be dispassionate, but this was difficult. My illusions over the years had been shattered. I had gone through the worst few weeks of my life. I have banished Walker completely from my mind. When I occasionally saw his name mentioned in the press or on advertising his films, I felt completely numb, but that is ethereal.

Fortunately, I am still enamoured with the game and have never given up my hidden desire to play for England against the Australians – day dreaming again I'm afraid. But what is left when one can't daydream?

Chapter 4

DEMON DRINK

I used to drink occasionally, usually on social occasions and mainly to keep in the swing of the crowd, but I never felt that it was an essential part of my life. I could take it or leave it. I always felt that I could be ebullient without artificial aids. However to some it was an essential part of life. It was natural to imbibe at every opportunity. In fact, I am sure that in some professions it was mandatory to be able to hold one's liquor. In banking at one time, the more that you could hold your drink, the higher you climbed in the industry. I don't suppose your capacity was part of your CV, but tests were done surreptitiously at social gatherings of bankers and your intake was noted by your superiors, and if you were on the verge of drunkenness, could still function, then you were considered for advancement.

For some years I was invited to a building society* golf day. Of the average twenty-four players, two were accountants and twenty-two bank managers. There was lunch and supper provided, but more importantly, half way around the course there was a bar set up and usually most competitors seemed to spend more time at that rendezvous than on the golf course

---

* An alternative financial institution to regular banks

itself. Knowing this, and the fact that I took the game reasonably seriously, I usually got to the club just prior to lunch.

On one occasion, the organisers introduced me to my companion for the game, who was propping up the bar. His immediate reaction to me was to say that I had missed valuable drinking time. However, we went into lunch with him holding a beer and a glass of gin to take with the meal.

He informed me that he was the local bank manager and had just spent the morning sharing a bottle of whiskey and vodka in his office with a client. Over the years – with other partners – this seemed the norm. Following the luncheon, he immediately sat up at the bar ready to be called to the first tee. I had made my excuses, and waited by the tee to watch others play off. Eventually my partner was called and we went off together.

It was a hot day and following various experiments to quench my thirst in the past, the only drink that would keep me reasonably cool was a flask of iced water that I always placed in my golf bag. When I took a sip, my partner inquired what I was drinking. When I mentioned my experiments and the fact that it was iced water, he seemed incredulous, and demanded that he try what I had.

He at once spat it out and said, "My God, you're right. You must be mad to drink that stuff."

"I told you so," I pointed out. I was upset that he did not believe me.

"That's sacrilege," he said, taking a flask out of his bag. "Try this," he demanded, which I did and my head began lifting from my shoulders.

"This is gin," I spluttered.

"Great, isn't it?" he said, as he took a deep slug.

The flask, which was quite large, seemed to hold over a bottle of the brew. From then on he continued to drink from the container until we came to the dreaded half way bar. He straightaway headed for that while I took a well-earned rest and tidied myself from the exertions of the morning of that hot day. I asked for orange juice, for which the bartender had to search high and low, as only alcohol seemed to be on the menu. Various couples passed us as I waited for my partner to drink the bar dry. Eventually, by gradual cajoling, I managed to tear him away and we went on our way. Surprisingly to me, he was playing better and better until we reached the end of the round. We showered and dressed.

I was taking my time, as I suspected that the inevitable would happen and I was not disappointed as he began harassing me to hurry up as we were missing valuable drinking time before supper. I told him to go ahead and found him just prior to entering the dining room for the meal, sitting on a bar stool with empty glasses in front of him. It seemed that there was a veritable cocktail cabinet of drinks lined up like massed ranks of the military before him. During supper, he continued drinking and of course when it came to the presentation of the prizes, the 'soak' had scooped first prize. This gave him the perfect excuse to celebrate his win with drink. Part of the tradition of the outing was that after supper a putting competition was held. I gave up the ghost and did not stay. I left him happily drinking himself into an early demise.

I did have alcoholic clients. One in particular suffered a severe stroke. In discussions with his consultant and mentioning his drinking habits, the consultant informed him in no uncertain manner that he must desist in his craving. My client pleaded with him that he could not stop his drinking habits. The consultant sympathetically told him that if he could not resist his craving, as far as he was concerned the only drink that had less potency was champagne. This was the lifeline my client wanted to hear. From then on he began drinking two or three bottles a day. Expensive though this was, it satisfied his longing and kept his equilibrium. He nevertheless died within a reasonably short time after the stroke, but in his own mind, he was at least back to his normal behaviour.

Another client invited me to a grand social gathering in a very expensive hotel in the West End of London. Although we were all dressed formally, within a short time after dinner the waiters wheeled in cockle* stalls and beer barrels and had transposed the magnificent dining room into an †East End street. The drinking and eating became serious. Bow ties and corsets were undone and hair was loosened. The whole tenure of the occasion changed from stiff-necked formality to complete abandon. After a short time, these well-dressed patrons were dropping in a drunken stupor and my client seriously informed me that he had already filled one leg with booze and was ready to fill the other, and then continue with his arms until his whole being was liquefied. That was the moment I left.

Charlie Weston was a motor trader, a good trader, if a little ruthless with his customers. If anyone had the temerity to ask him – after buying a car – whether there was a guarantee given, his stock answer was 'Yea' to the end of the road'. He eventually decided to change the whole trading aspect of his company and concentrate on expensive vehicles. However, his attitude did not change to his potential customers. The moment he sold a vintage car he would immediately inform the purchaser that the petrol station was just around the corner. I informed him that a friend of mine had purchased a Rolls Royce from a well-known West End dealer, and when it was delivered to his home by a liveried chauffeur, the whole back seat of the car was covered in flowers.

It appealed to the lady of the house, who insisted that when her husband decided to change the vehicle he had to go

---

* Shell fish
† Considered to be a poorer part of London

67

to the same dealer. Charlie however, pooh-poohed the idea and stated that he did not wish to charge his customers excessively for this nonsense. He was happy with his own mark up. I could not convince him of the psychological advantage he could gain. Charlie was bluff in his business and was not the suave salesman, encountered elsewhere, that I expected him to be. He was happy with his dealing methods and was down to earth. Outside of his trade, he was the most charming and engaging fellow one could meet – generous to a fault, remembering his background. He was, what is known in that parlance as a 'rough diamond'. A man who could drink his way through a vineyard, or a brewery with ease, whatever his tipple. He was not biased in his intake of liquor. Apart from methalated spirits, anything was acceptable unless it was either water or soft drinks, which were an anathema to him.

One day he invited me to lunch with his bank manager and said he would collect me from my office, then take me to the restaurant for the meeting. Well of course, we did not go straight to the restaurant, but to a bar in the city. The bank manager was introduced to me, and after the usual pleasantries and introductions, drinks were ordered. I did not drink, therefore ordered tomato juice. Eyebrows were raised at my request and a look of disdain came over both of them, and I'm sure over the rest of the drinkers in the bar. After all what is a bar for? I stuck to my guns and the juice was reluctantly given to me without a word. My client and manager stuck to gin and tonics. By the time we left the bar, I counted that for every drink that they ordered and I matching them with juice, I had drunk fourteen tomato juices. This made me feel worse than they did. The restaurant then beckoned, and at lunch, there was already six bottles of wine on the table. I then gave up the tomato juice – I couldn't fancy another one – and switched to orange juice as an alternative. Naturally, the bottles of wine were swiftly consumed, and following a reasonably excellent lunch, brandies were ordered and drunk with relish from my two companions. At about 3:30 p.m. we left. I then looked for a taxi whilst my client and his bank manager were hugging each other and saying goodbye.

My client insisted that he take me back to my office in his car. I protested vehemently and warned him of the dangers of drink driving and that he had drunk too much. He accused me of being sanctimonious and said that he was quite able to drive and that the drink had not affected his powers of concentration one jot. On reflection, I should have informed the authorities of the situation, but I was a coward and my client was such a nice fellow. He could have lost his licence and therefore his business. I reluctantly entered the Mercedes and he started up the vehicle and slowly drew away from the curb. I was sitting next to him with my eyes partly closed and praying that a) we would not have an accident, b) that the police did not notice and c) that the journey back to the office would be more sedate than a funeral procession. I glanced at Charlie and he seemed quite normal, just concentrating a bit harder. However, as we drove along the Strand in London, he began weaving across the road – ever so slightly, but enough for me to notice.

"Charlie," I said. "What are you doing?"

With an enigmatic smile playing around his lips he said. "I'm getting the birds[*] in the target."

As you know, Mercedes cars have their emblem on the bonnet[†] of their cars, a circle within, which were presumably three propellers or whatever. This therefore was the target. That was the end; I insisted he drop me there and then. Of course, abuse followed my request.

"Perry, I said I would take you to your office and I will."

---

[*] English slang referring to girls
[†] The 'bonnet' is the hood of the car in England

I closed my eyes and did not pray, as I thought that the Almighty was already dealing with wars, starvation and pestilence, and my pleas would have gone to the back of a list of important work that he had to do. So eventually we arrived at my office, thankfully in one piece. I happily bade farewell to my client and staggered into the building. I did telephone him later and he was as bright as a button, as if everything was fine and he felt wonderful; he said that after a lie down he would probably go to the pub. His feelings were the antithesis to my feelings after all those juices I had consumed, and I remembered the old maxim never to mix one's drinks, as I had done with tomato and orange. Excessive drinking must be in the genes, for sometime later I was involved with Charlie's brother Jimmy, naturally as a client.

One weekend, I was walking along a high street in north London with my father-in-law (of blessed memory) who was a man of supreme elegance, even to wearing spats. Naturally he had a bowler hat, perfectly brushed and a velvet collar on his overcoat – the epitome of the well-dressed man. We had been to a religious ceremony and were on the way to his home for lunch. Even I was dressed appropriately. We were talking seriously and in depth and as we passed a row of shops, suddenly and without warning, a door opened and two men fell out onto the pavement in front of us.

One looked up from his prone position and with a scream shouted, "Perry," and looked directly up to me.

My father-in-law gave me a withering look and said, "Do you know this blaggard? Please say that you don't." This summing up was typical of his general demeanour. I hesitantly replied that unfortunately I did.

Jimmy rose with difficulty with his partner, breathed an alcoholic haze over me and tried to grab my shoulders.

"Come with us," he requested. I demurred.

"I don't think so, Jimmy, I'm going to this gentleman's flat for lunch." He blinkingly stared at me.

"You've got to come and bring the old man with you." My father-in-law looked at me, and then at those two sizzled gentlemen with disdain.

"If these gentlemen," and he emphasised the word 'gentlemen', "wish you to go with them, you may do so if you desire."

I protested vehemently that I wanted to go with him to lunch. Jimmy and his partner protested that I had to go with them, my father-in-law waved in a perfunctory manner and strolled away, saying he would see me later.

The partners grabbed my elbows and steered me towards the door of the shop, which led to a private bar. They immediately plied me with drinks, particularly whiskey – glasses of it despite my continuous protests. My complaints were immediately ignored. The drinks piled up on the bar and empty glasses were strewn over the alcohol spilled counter. I do not know how many snifters I had, all I know is that I was now more sozzled than my clients. Eventually I was released from their clutches after a dizzying time and tried desperately to remember where I was and where I was supposed to be going. I sat on the curb outside the club with my head in my hands, continuously saying to myself, 'where am I going and supposed to be'. Shoppers walking by, because I was dressed reasonably well, showed a certain amount of sympathy and tried to ask me if I was well. I'm sure that if I were shabby I would have at least got a kick in the back and pushed over. People are kind to those that on the surface look respectable.

A hazy memory of lunch in a flat[*] came to the fore and I slowly rose and headed slowly, and with care, to the flat. Fortunately, this was only a short distance away from where I

---

[*] Apartment

71

had been ambushed. Ambushed? More likely kidnapped with dire circumstances, punishable by a long prison sentence. I kept my finger on the bell of the flat and when the door was opened, I stumbled through the hall to the dining room in trepidation, and with glazed eyes surveyed the room. I knew that lunch had finished, mainly because the dining table was free of any encumbrances, and the fact that the guests were staring at me in astonishment and a certain amount of disgust. I was drunk, and it showed. My clothes were in disarray and my eyes bleary. I stood, or rather swayed, holding onto a chair and without a word tried to turn on my heel and leave for the bedroom, where I collapsed on the bed fully dressed and slept for hours, waking the next day with a head that was full of leaking dynamite and a force nine gale sickness. The whole incident was horrendous. The only saving grace was that on the following Monday I was still trying to assemble some form of equilibrium to myself, and the telephone rang to inform me that Jimmy was calling. He came on to apologise for what had happened over the weekend and that applied to his partner. I demurred and accepted his words of contrition, but informed him that if it would happen again (Lord forbid) I would not be responsible for my actions. Usually it is a fact that women drive men to drink, but in this instance it was brothers.

Chapter 5

TWITCHING CURTAINS

My uncle Larry was a 'card'. He and his wife were bright, exuberant and 'life lovers'. When I was a child I was the only nephew feted and spoiled by them. This couple inspired me with their unbounded happiness and greeted me with enthusiasm and love when I stayed with them for a week or so. I adored staying with them, particularly as they always owned a dog, which I was not allowed, and as an animal lover this was heaven to me. I was treated as their child, as throughout their life they were childless. Both of them were reasonably small and my aunt Laura was petite and attractive. They loved ballroom dancing and tried without success to impart this enthusiasm to me, but to no avail as I learned from an early age that I suffered from two left feet. However, I did enjoy watching them glide over the dance floor and as they passed me they always smiled and nodded. Although I was one of only a few children at the 'Palais[*], I nevertheless loved the atmosphere and the beat of the orchestra.

Going to their home afterwards in their little car was a great treat, particularly as my own family never owned a vehicle. Being greeted by the dog and my aunt offering me any

---

[*] Dance Hall in England

73

food that I wished was a dream. When I left them to go to my own home and parents, my emotions were extremely mixed. I missed their spoiling of me, their laughter and of course their dog.

Larry at one time worked near my home and would come regularly for lunch. He always brightened the meal and I vividly remember at one luncheon, I shook the ketchup bottle without realising the top was not fixed correctly; the tomato sauce flew over my uncle and he was drenched in the red sticky substance. My parents glowered at me, and any other person would have been extremely annoyed and would have called me a 'silly boy', but not Larry, he burst out laughing, and could not stop, ruffled my hair and said 'what a great trick'. The barriers were broken and my parents, even if they wanted to, could not admonish me. Such was his outlook and demeanour. My aunt and uncle brightened my mundane, childish life.

Then, for no apparent reason, after some years of employment they decided to go self-employed and inexplicably purchased a corner shop in London. Not up north where they proliferated, but in the metropolis – a shop that sold everything from candles to bags of sugar; a small general store, which entailed long hours and hard work – as those stores still do now, where they exist in competition against the super store, but with an added personal service and range of products for their customers. This was before the superstore and their indifference to the public. Asking about family problems and sympathizing, celebrating with their clientele and knowing them intimately were part of trading with corner shops. For this purpose my aunt and uncle sold their little house to purchase the shop and moved into the shop's upper part and back parlour. The shop was not, unfortunately, situated in a salubrious part of town and therefore their customers were good ordinary folk who paid up on their purchases and occasionally requested credit. My uncle of course refused credit, informing his customers that it was a shop and not a bank. This was accepted in good faith and the customer's purchases were restricted to their expenditure needs. This was before supermarkets, where credit cards can be used. The purchase of even a box of matches was thought about and the purchase of a tin of ham was a major decision. Thus the margins of profit were small and the business relied on turnover.

Larry, who had been quite a heavy smoker, realised that for every cigarette that he smoked, he had to sell a packet of twenty. To help his craving, he immediately stopped the habit. Consequently he and my aunt's attitude changed in all things. They became dull and money oriented; dancing and all other happy pursuits were dismissed as a waste of money. Everything was gauged in profit. For every pound that they could spend, they had to take fifteen pounds in the shop. Further, these pursuits would take them away from the shop and thus lose turnover. In other words, their whole personalities changed. Every penny they spent was converted in their mind to turnover. The calculations they made over personal money spent was of mathematical proportions. Even bare necessities were scrutinised, and although they could be taken from the shelves of the shop, there was reluctance to go down that road. Money was to be spent in small quantities and therefore customers would have had to spend more in the shop. Their waking lives were spent conjuring up schemes to this end; a complete contrast to their previous 'devil may care' attitude. I was inevitably expected, as their nephew, to be their accountant to the business. I reluctantly accepted this dubious honour on the basis that they had given me a fabulous time when I was a child and that they still had a dog. However, this time their reasoning was that it was no longer a pet as such, but a necessity for security on their premises.

There was one particular change in my uncle and that was that he had become shrewd and devious – a complete antithesis to his 'throw away' attitude in the past. His shrewdness was simply illustrated one day when he was driving away from the wholesalers and was involved in a car accident. He immediately realised that although he carried car insurance, this did not cover him for 'carriage of goods', which would have cost him an additional higher insurance premium. He therefore, with presence of mind, immediately drove away, but looking into his rearview mirror saw that the car with which he had the accident was following him. He accelerated and took immediate evasive action, cutting down side streets and crossing junctions with the car still following him. This was becoming serious. Eventually the following driver cut in front of Larry and made him pull up. This was a very nervous situation for him, and as the driver approached, excuses and reasons were vying with each other in Larry's brain.

The driver knocked on my uncle's window, which he reluctantly wound down and stared at him, white faced.

"Are you going to the police to report the accident?" the driver asked.

"Well," Larry hesitated. The driver had a pleading look on his face.

"Don't do that," he stated.

"I was banned from driving and have only a few more weeks to go before I can drive again. I only drove because it was an emergency. Otherwise, of course I would not have driven." This was an answer to Larry's prayers. He was worried because he was not insured and having an accident with a banned driver was his salvation. Larry put on a serious expression.

"Frankly, I was on my way to report the fracas, but by the way you look, distraught and concerned," he stated. "Perhaps I might be slightly hasty." The other driver breathed a sigh of relief.

"I've had a look at the damage to your car," he said after walking around my uncle's vehicle, and at the same time pulling a wad of notes from his pocket and pulling off a few notes. "How much do you think your repairs would be?" he asked.

My uncle, putting on a grave face, said, "Of course you realise I shouldn't be a party to this, however to ease your problem and if you could assure me that you won't drive until your ban is lifted, I suppose it will do no harm." Larry then mentioned some astronomical figure, which the driver with simpering thanks paid him the amount and immediately drove off.

As far as Larry was concerned, this was a great 'double whammy'. He was not caught for uninsured driving and had made a large profit on the repairs.

This incident illustrated in sharp relief the mindset of my uncle – money was all-important. The accumulation became the zenith of their lives. They continued in this vein for some years and then suddenly, without warning, they decided to sell the business, retire and move to the east coast. We could not fathom this couple, from leading happy and contented lives, through the money grabbing period of shop keeping, and then the sudden decision to sell up and retire. Of course they had no ties with family and therefore the decisions that they made were capable of being made. There was only the two of them and they did not have to consider anyone else. Larry and Laura were 'footloose' and could live and plan their lives as they wished.

When they sold the business, and on the day before they were leaving, they summoned me to collect their account books, boxes of invoices and receipts to finalise their tax affairs. I collected them, albeit with a certain pleasure on my part, as being their accountant was a nightmare. They never collated any of their bills, although their account records were fairly good. They always left me with the task of sorting out their boxes of paperwork and with the fee that I charged them at the time, took up more of my staff's work than was normal.

Nevertheless, the deed was done and the work finished. There were a number of boxes and invoices, and as they had moved from London, for me to return them by post to their new house, this would have entailed considerable expense, so I stored them for a while, hoping that on their next visit to London I could transfer everything for them to take back to the coast.

Weeks went by, and as they seemed reluctant to journey to my office to collect their belongings, and as the boxes were taking up room in my storage, I hit on a brilliant idea. Well, it was brilliant at the time. The idea was that I would pile the boxes in my car with my family and visit our relatives on the coast. This I know, smacked of Mohammed and the mountain, but I looked upon it as a day out away from the drudgery of the office, and to see how they were getting on in their new surroundings – also to see whether they still had a dog. As it was a guard dog, perhaps that was sold with the business and they had acquired a more domesticated animal.

When I broached the idea with my family they were enthusiastic. My mother, who was Larry's sister, was also enlisted for the journey. This, I thought at the time, was a stroke of genius, as the two of them had not communicated regularly since Larry had moved. There was no animosity between them, it was just that the cost of the telephone call from a distance of approximately thirty miles might have deemed prohibitive to my aunt and uncle.

We journeyed to the coast and after a grand time on the beach, funfairs, promenade walks and an excellent lunch we decided to call on my relatives. Incidentally – and this was a further stroke of genius – we had packed teabags and biscuits and would therefore only demand from Larry and Laura the use of their cups and water, thus giving them an excuse for no refusal. On second thoughts, I should have packed milk powder and some plastic crockery as an emergency, but then again I was doing them an injustice. Surely we weren't asking for tea at the 'Ritz'[*], just to help with out sustenance, the demands being of a minimal nature.

So we arrived at this neat little bungalow with a flowered walkway to a front door which was covered with frosted glass. I walked up the path on my own, leaving the family in the car, and rang the doorbell. I heard a young dog yapping and was pleased. There was no answer and I rang again and waited. There was no reply again and I reluctantly walked back to the car. Sod it! I had to take his parcels back to the office, what a bind. Just then my wife told me that she saw a shadow cross the glass door. I pooh-pooed the idea, but she insisted that she had seen something and I was instructed to return, which I did and rang the bell again.

The dog yapped again, but there was no reply. I returned to the car, where I was informed that the same shadow had crossed the glass door. There was slight panic in my wife's insistence that I should make a reconnaissance of the property and see if there were any problems. I inquired of her what problem could there be? She naturally thought of the worst, that our relatives had been burgled. The thieves, finding our relations on the premises, bludgeoned them and left them tied to chair whilst the bungalow was being ransacked. Too many crime novels must have made their mark on her imagination. She further insisted that when I searched the back of the premises to look for signs of entry.

I tried to be positive and pointed out that if Larry and Laura were prostrate, the dog, being I assumed of an affectionate nature, would be pining by the bodies and not barking at the door. As an afterthought I also pointed out, in my cool calculating brain, that if the thieves were still in the house and found me wandering about, I would be their third victim.

---

[*] Top hotel in London

This suggestion was totally ignored and I walked up the path again and began walking hesitantly around the property. The dog started barking. Everything to my unpracticed eye seemed to be in order, except for a small window being open high up on the property. I went back and imparted this news to the family, whereupon my son, who was getting more excited over the dastardly deed that had been committed, also informed me that he had seen a shadow. Oh no, he's caught the air of the intrigue bug as well, or his imagination had taken flight. My mum, who was more down to earth, also confirmed the sighting, but as she adored my son, there could be bias there. At this point, with added bravado – as I had returned safely from my sojourn with the devils in the bungalow – I exclaimed.

"Stuff and nonsense." I was now getting tired and hungry and insisted that we drive away. As we turned the corner my wife noticed a telephone box and demanded that I stop the car and dial 999.[*]

"What for?" I demanded.

"There is definitely something wrong at the house," my wife exclaimed. "Your family bound and bleeding to death, and you're not interested?"

"Of course, I'm somewhat concerned, but I have a reputation to uphold and do not wish to be prosecuted for wasting police time," I felt snooty.

"That's absolute rubbish!" she admonished and continued, "If you're too weak or uncaring, I will do it."

"Okay," I said, and entered the telephone box and reluctantly telephoned the police. I explained to the operator that we had called on my relations, finding no reply and seeing shadows cross the door. Details were given and I got back to the car. Within minutes there was the sound of sirens and a

---

[*] Police emergency number

police car screeched to a halt outside their bungalow. In a quiet coastal hamlet, normally sleepy and benign came a constant stream of people, some curious, others excited and some to pass the time of day, and a plethora of children intent on joining in the fun. It was amazing where all the people had come from. There was babble from the crowd, which seemed to number at least fifty residents, together with their dogs and prams, all staring at the police, the property and us.

The policeman came over to me and inquired whether I had made the call and I reluctantly answered that I had, feeling apprehensive. One policeman then went up the path to the front door, while the other went to inspect the property. The policeman that went to the front door was more mature than his colleague and rang the bell. Lo and behold, the door opened and my uncle stood there.

The policeman looked at him and then looked at me, with a glance of sympathy, and said, "Do you know this gentleman, Sir?"

I was blazing and replied immediately. "No!" My uncle went white.

"But Perry it's me," he pleaded. The policeman gave me a quizzical look and started fiddling with his handcuffs.

My aunt came to the door with the small dog barking by her side. "Perry, tell them who we are," she begged.

The policeman looked at me again with a grin. I felt as if I could carry on this charade right up to the eventual court case, which would ensue. I thought that a night in the cells would do them no harm, but this would involve me seeing them again in the dock, and standing in the witness box trying to put them away. However, this was a delicious moment, which I wanted to savour, but then I noticed my mother, Larry's sister, looking disappointed and despondent.

I hesitated a bit longer and blurted out to the policeman. "Well, officer. He has a resemblance to a gentleman that I know. However, the woman with him is more familiar to me."

Proudly I was offered the policeman's hand as he left with his associate, telling me in front of my relatives that I had done the right thing.

The crowd dispersed, upset and annoyed that there was no murder to be witnessed. Some glared at my uncle. It was very embarrassing for him, for he had to live amongst them and would forever be tainted with his stupidity and obduracy to acknowledge his relatives and offer them succour in their predicament. However, he took on a dominant air.

"Why the hell did you call the police?" he demanded. Of course the best line of defense is attack, but I was not going to stand for that.

"We have come a fair distance to see you and just to return your records. Your sister is in the car, and together with my family. We did not propose to cadge any refreshments from you and for your information I have our tea with us." I was still fuming. "I want you to come to the car and collect your papers and be done with it."

Larry sheepishly followed me to the vehicle, attempting to acknowledge his sister and requested that we go inside the property for a chat. No tea mind, just an invitation to talk. This was refused 'out of hand' and he strolled back up the drive carrying his records, boxes of invoices and account books. I naturally did not help him as he struggled with his goods. Before we left, I just had time to bend down and pet his new dog. Of course it goes without question that the animal was completely innocent in the debacle.

We then drove away, later having a 'slap up' afternoon tea at a hotel and I dropping the cups, teabags and biscuits into a waste bin with a feeling of good riddance.

Chapter 6

WHAT'S IN A NAME

In my practice I had to come up with names for companies. It is felt that a trading name is sacrosanct. It must be catchy and to the point. Short names were usually considered the best. Even well known names from trading companies have in the past changed their names, as they were conceived to be too long when they started. One can look up old records of very popular companies and find that the original name had been changed, or altered to fit into modern parlance. This was done to make them more acceptable and in particular, remembered. In recent times, names that were familiar to the public have been changed at great expense. The idea now is to fit the logo to the name, or visa versa.

I always considered that the choosing of a company name laid the foundation for its future trading. As individuals, we have the right through legal means – for example Deeds of Poll or usage – to change the name that we are born with. Parents can be inconsiderate in naming their children. A name given to a child at birth, which is ideal for a child, can seem ridiculous when they become an adult. The amount of cute names given to children of those in the entertainment business will look damn silly when they are adults. However, this trend is not fashionable and passes a phase. It is inevitable that in the future more mundane names will proliferate and we will get back to normality.

One of my personal triumphs for the motor industry was to incorporate the word 'carriage' in the title. This I felt gave certain gravitas to the traders. Although high-powered cars were sold under that title and not just 'old bangers'[*], customers felt that they were purchasing cars of quality and vintage. There was an air of solidity in the title. Whether the cars were sold from a back street or from Mayfair[†], reliability and style was in the name. I always, told prospective businesses that even before finances, premises and all that goes with starting a business, they had to think of a name for the company as a first priority. The first reaction was always: so what's in a name? I then had to explain that once the name was decided upon and acceptable, the work would then commence.

Thus Harry and Mark came to see me concerning the partnership that they had and wished to be incorporated into a company. Harry and Mark had begun their partnership of selling second-hand cars from way back, from post war bombsites and had graduated to small premises in North London. This consisted of a prefabricated office on an open site, surrounded by barbed wire netting and sufficient space to hold six cars at a squeeze. They felt that incorporating their partnership into a company would give them a certain prestige. This idea was fairly typical of some businesses. The main reason for having a company was usually to cover the partners from prospective bankruptcy, but in a lot of cases this was not the reason. Most people in business thought that putting the word 'limited' in the name showed that the company was solid. This was psychological more than business acumen.

Harry and Mark had traded reasonably successfully for some years as 'H.M. CARS' and this name converted to 'H.M.

---

[*] Old cars
[†] Top area of London

CARS LTD'. I thought at the time, 'Wow! What time and brainpower had the two used to come up with that catchy name?' They must have spent days considering it. However, they instructed me to file documents for the incorporation, which I did and immediately forgot about the papers. Some weeks later, my clients telephoned me and inquired as to the progress of their application. I telephoned the appropriate authority, which was Company's House*, which deal with company formations and registrations and was informed by them that the documents were still in the pipeline and would be dealt with shortly. As to timescale, they seemed very casual and promised that with current registrations and red tape, the matter would be dealt with. A week or so after my request, my secretary informed me that there was a personal call for me, and that the caller refused to give his name and would only speak to me. Normally I did not want to speak to anyone unless a name was given, and the purpose of their call was divulged, but I took the call.

"Mr. St. John?" This semi-cultured voice came on the telephone.

"Yes," I answered reluctantly.

"Well I'm Detective Inspector Webb of the Special Branch[†]," he said. Special Branch? Good Lord! What had I done? I mentally went over my past. I knew that in the dim and distant past I had East European relatives. I also at one time, felt that I should have been a spy and went no further in my desires. Perhaps I was being offered a job in the Security Services. As I child I knew that to write letters in invisible ink, one could use milk and when the letter was dry, place it in front of heat and miraculously, brown smudges would be revealed

---

[*] Hall of Records in England

[†] A very select division of the English Police force that investigates security matters

and the letter in part read. However, I did not feel that bit of skullduggery would suffice.

James Bond films were coming to prominence and in a fleeting moment I had met one of the producers. All said and done, I had no connection with MI5[*]. Further, I was not of an insignificant size or demeanour to shadow someone or hide amongst the crowds. Apart from the letter writing, I had to admit I had no special skills. I knew that I would probably make a hash of any assignment, especially over the fact that I could not keep my mouth shut for long and secrets would explode all over the place. I was now nervous, but curious.

"So Detective Inspector Webb, what can I do for you?" I said hesitantly.

"I would like to visit you on a somewhat delicate matter," was his reply.

I had visions of the Royal Family instructing me to look after their substantial finances. Or my other alternative thought was that the Chancellor of the Exchequer[†] required my expertise for a forthcoming budget. Various high fluting ideas played around my head until the meeting. At this stage I tried to think of a way of charging a respectable fee for my time, but discarded this in favour of a peerage[‡] or at the very least a knighthood[§]. That would be my recompense. If they should wish to pay me out of the Civil Purse, that would be a further bonus.

Webb came to my office on time and was ushered into my room. He was smartly dressed and had what I presumed to be an army regimental tie neatly knotted. He was tall and languid, removed his trilby hat and after shaking hands with a firm grip, presented me with his visiting card, sat before me at

---

[*] British security service
[†] Head of the government treasury
[‡] "Lord"
[§] "Sir"

my desk and spoke, "Mr. St. John, I understand that you are forming a company for your clients called 'H.M. Cars Ltd.', is that right?" I nodded in agreement and was even more curious.

He continued, "You know of course that this name could be construed as 'Her Majesty'. You know, 'H.M.' and all that?"

"Her Majesty?" I blurted out.

"Yes Mr. St. John. If not Her Majesty, at least the government." He became serious. "Well?"

I grinned.

"The moment the Queen, or the government start selling cars from a measly office in North London, that will be the time to emigrate." Webb became serious. "This is no joke, Mr. St. John." He admonished me. "There could be various implications involved."

"What implications?" I asked, trying desperately to stop from laughing out loud.

"The implication that there could be an assumption that in some minor way there was approval or backing for this venture from government sources."

He was serious! Good Lord, what have we come to – bureaucracy gone mad?

"The documents I have filed show the names and addresses of the directors. Surely you have checked these and found that they have no connections to any higher authority and that they are just hard working boys trying to make a living. The name of the company came about by using the initials of their first names, Harry and Mark." I was now getting somewhat peeved. No Peerage or Knighthood, and now more importantly no fees or prestige. All my wishes dashed in one fell swoop.

Webb looked at me for some time without speaking and then said, "Of course we did check their backgrounds. As a compromise, can't they reverse the name and call it 'M & H Cars Ltd?"

Now I wasn't going to be pressurised after my hopes were so severely dashed.

"No," I said vehemently.

"That is the name that they have chosen and that is the name they want. Incidentally they took weeks to think of that particular name, so why should they go through the process and time-consuming worry by being pressurised by you or your superiors?"

Webb showed a flash of anger at my reply and got up to go. His parting shot was that I would be wise to heed his suggestion and that I would hear from him in due course. He said that I would expect that the name would probably be accepted. I breathed a sigh of relief. I did not know whether to laugh or to hysterically laugh. The whole incident seemed bizarre. It would seem that some minor official in Companies House had reported the request to Scotland Yard and they, in an officious manner, took the registration seriously enough to appoint a detective inspector rather than a detective constable to deal with the matter. I was of the opinion that the whole situation had got out of hand. I then heard that the name would be registered and informed my clients. I did not discuss the visit as it seemed too ridiculous to relate and perhaps I would be considered paranoid.

Some years later, Harry and Mark visited me to discuss the purchase of a small property that they wished to convert into furnished flats. They informed me that this was just the start and eventually more properties would be bought, with the object of giving up the car business and staying in the property business. They instructed me to form another company, and as their present company had been reasonably successful, they wanted to register 'H.M. PROPERTIES LTD'. I tried to dissuade them, but they were adamant, so we filed the papers. After a few weeks, my secretary was on the telephone to me saying that there was a personal caller who would not give their name. I knew what was coming. The semi-cultured voice came on.

"Mr. St. John, perhaps you remember me. I am Detective Chief Inspector Webb." I was ready.

"Congratulations Detective Chief Inspector Webb on your promotion. I hope that this was through your diligent work in the force, and not because of the successful conclusion of our past meeting." Webb ignored my sarcasm.

"Are you playing bloody games with us?" he asked.

"No," I said. "But my answer is the same as I gave you before. That when Her Majesty or the Government purchase a house in South London, and convert this into flats, I will have my bags packed."

"I do not appreciate your sarcasm, Mr. St. John." However, I could detect slight humour in his voice. "But as you have explained, I will let it go through, but please convey to your clients that this is the end and I don't wish to see you and your applications for similar names to be applied," he remarked.

I thought about this for a moment. "I will assure you that I will not suggest those initials again. However, I might, and say might, put forward names like for instance 'C & E' (Customs & Excise) if I have clients called Charlie and Eddie." Webb snorted and put down the telephone.

That was my minor brush with part of the Security Services and must admit after being cheeky to Webb, I was sure that for a few weeks I was followed, my telephone tapped and mail opened. But that couldn't happen, or could it?

Chapter 7

SHOCK AND HORROR

For those that still remember and for historians, the 1950's were still a time of austerity. Although the Second World War had been over for a few years, nevertheless, food and goods were still rationed. Many items were still in short supply. Men and women, who had been purloined by the government to fight the war, were now civilians, all endeavouring to recapture the pre-war standards – not the poverty, but the values that permeated Great Britain in that era. The civilian population released from purgatory, distractions and horrors of the war years tried desperately to return to some form of normality – some with success, others unfortunately not. Many easily settled into a reasonable routine while others found the transition difficult.

There were considerable problems in re-establishing themselves in the aftermath of conflict – what is now regarded and recognised as post-traumatic stress and to a certain extent is sparingly treated. Nevertheless, the fortunate few could discard their uniforms and return to the routine they were used to prior to serving their country. Many were fostering pre-war ethics, manners and morality. The 'city gent' returned, somewhat battered. The housewives put their pinnies back on and began to struggle to provide sustenance for the family. The workers donned their dungarees and went back to the machines they had cared for lovingly, and to turn them into peaceful pursuits and not the mass manufacturing of arms. Normality, such as it was, was hesitantly returning, but with renewed vigour. Morality with winning the war was in the ascendancy. It was given the utmost priority amongst the government and the people. It was expected that everyone would put this as his or her top priority to counteract the moral decline in the war years. Sexuality was frowned upon following the promiscuity that was prevalent during those years. The reason now was that everyone was going to live a long and fruitful life, and that the sexual revolution of the years of war – when drink was prevalent on the basis that it could be the last time before death struck – no longer applied.

It was in this period that as a young man, I tentatively started my accountancy practice. I will not bemoan the pain of difficulties I encountered, but tried in my small way to establish my practice, waiting and hoping for prospective clients to call upon me for my professional advice and help. It was in this atmosphere that Mr. William Bartholomew came to see me. He was a man of about forty-five, strong physically, but I felt, weak in demeanour and behaviour. When I met him he had very sad eyes and a downtrodden air. I proffered him a seat and asked him his problem.

"It's like this, Mr. St. John. I have this summons from the Inland Revenue* Commissioners to attend them at a hearing." With that he passed the paper to me, which I glanced at and noticed that the meeting would be held in a reasonably smart market town.

To explain, the Income Tax Commissioners were a body of men, usually businessmen of the local community and chaired by an Inspector of Taxes. They met on a regular basis and their particular function was to hear appeals against Income Tax Assessments of tax claimed. They sat regularly and were guided through the intricacies of Income Tax laws and

---

* The equivalent in England of the IRS in the United States

91

appeals by the chairman. They were lay people, and their main function was presumably to use their common sense when it came to adjournments and whether to grant time to the taxpayer to supply the relevant information or to – and this was difficult – to refuse a time limit. The impression that the taxpayer or his representative gave to the panel was of the utmost importance.

I, in training, had only been to one appeal, which was not very enlightening. So when I was reviewing this summons, I was thinking whether I should refuse the assignment. However, the lack of finance at the time made me make my mind up quickly and I said, "Oh, Mr. Bartholomew, I can deal with this for you. Have no worries on that score."

I had the chutzpah[*] of youth. I was not qualified to do this, but what the hell! One had to learn, even if it's off the back of someone else. Unlike a new surgeon, who's first cut on a human being can cause death, my inexperience would only cause my client money. Thus it was of no consequence.

I continued, "Can you tell me what you do for a living, Mr. Bartholomew?" He looked at me, with what I thought was a tear in his eye.

"I did have a newsagent and tobacconists with my wife," and he mentioned the town that he was in. "Mr. St. John," he continued. "My wife has left me."

I waited for him to settle himself and said, "I'm sorry to hear that."

My sympathy was tempered, as I was engaged and was naturally under the impression that couples stayed together for life. How naive! But in those far off days, very few couples broke up. They stuck together because of children, and it was considered an infamous act to divorce or separate. Apart from

_____

[*] Yiddish for being somewhat arrogant

92

that, it was expensive to get a divorce and there was a certain attitude to couples that had parted, usually of a derogatory nature to outsiders – 'no smoke without fire'. The woman was a hussy and the man a philanderer.

"Because of that, I have neglected to deal with my tax returns and frankly Mr. St. John, my life has fallen apart," he said glumly.

"I appreciate that Mr. Bartholomew and I understand," I said sadly. "But you must stick to your obligations". He looked at me again.

"I know that, but the circumstances have been traumatic."

I conjectured. Did she run away to sea? Did she join the Army? Was she captured and held for ransom? Or perish the thought, for the slave market? No, not that last!

My client was about forty-five and his wife must've been only a few years less. I assumed that the slave marketers only wanted nubile girls and she probably did not fit the bill. My mind was running away with itself. I decided to grab the moment.

"Do you know where she is?" I asked.

"Oh yes," he answered. "She is living with another woman, a long time friend of hers."

"So she will come back to you, I'm sure. She just wanted a break from, in her mind, a mundane life," I conjectured.

"No, that's wrong. She is living with this lady as a lover," he answered, with I must admit, certain frankness. I tried another tack. This whole situation was getting out of hand.

"That's only your assumption," I said. "Have you any proof?"

"Of course. Not only has she told me herself, but I also have had it somewhat confirmed by her neighbours. In fact, the whole street is whispering about it."

This was a shock to me; homosexuality between males was not tolerated in the country and by the government. There were laws concerning this aspect and any man importuning another individual, or as they say, had lewd relations were subject to the full penalty of the law. This was common knowledge, but between women there did not seem any law or disapproval. It must have been that men did not acknowledge, or accept that such things were going on. It was thought that women should only wish to be with men. Male ego was dominant. A woman had to have a man; it was incumbent upon them to follow this course. Men would not tolerate women who did not consider anything else. Of course, they could show their affection to animals regardless of their sex, but not to want to be with a man was a shameful sin. In the 1950's, it was still predominately a man's world. Women were assumed, and expected, to be subservient to a man's will.

"This puts a different complexion on your case for an adjournment, Mr. Bartholomew. I'm not too sure the commissioners will accept your assertion. And I emphasise that your wife is a... I hesitated, "Lesbian," which I think is the word. "And having a lesbian affair with another woman," I continued.

I put on a stern manner, but looking at my client's downcast expression, I smiled.

"I'm sorry, but I think it's best to tell the truth and shock the commissioners to accept your situation. I shall be pleased to represent you at the hearing, but when I meet you, you must promise me that you will have all your records with you. Do that and we can get cracking straight away with settling your affairs. That is, of course, tax affairs," I chortled.

Mr. Bartholomew agreed and we made an arrangement to meet outside the offices of the town hall prior to the meeting, at which time he would pay my expenses for the day and part of my prospective fee. I took the train to town on the allotted day – with certain trepidation I must admit, for I was going into unknown territory and was going to shock the old fogies. I assumed that they would be old fogies, or at least somewhat considerably older than myself. At that time, in my youth anyone over forty-five was an old man. The shock I was proposing would change their placid existence down to their cotton socks. It was quite a challenge. Either way they could refuse the adjournment on the basis that my excuse to them was too preposterous, or that I, a whippersnapper, had the temerity to be before them with this 'made up' story.

I met Mr. Bartholomew and perfunctorily asked about his well-being and was assured by him that he felt relieved that the time had come; we entered the town hall. In most market towns and metropolitan towns, town halls were the epitome of nineteenth-century extravagant architecture. There was abundant marble, carvings, fine wood, columns, corridors, offices, towers and anything a flamboyant architect can impose on a building for the purpose of administrating the town's finances. The mere fact that the cost of these buildings came from the wages of hard working people, who were residents in the town, was of no consequence in considering the over priced buildings and as such no expense was spared.

The building that we entered was of this imposing structure. We entered through a vast entrance leading to a magnificent hallway, high and with similar pillars to those outside. There was a marble floor, which if you were not careful in your step, could cause serious injury over its highly cleaned floor in black and white slabs. You did have to be careful. Naturally there was a sign that the council would not be responsible for any injuries sustained by carelessness on behalf of the taxpayers, a further hazard to be overcome.

Mr. Bartholomew and myself sat in the corridor waiting to be called. There were other taxpayers and their accountants waiting, some apprehensively, others exuding confidence. There was a heavy pall of cigarette smoke in the area and the council, in their wisdom, had supplied ashtrays; although this was reasonably early in the day, the ashtrays were already overflowing with cigarette ends, thus showing the concern and in some cases fear of those waiting. I endeavoured to put on the air of a seasoned pro; my client nervously twiddled his thumbs and occasionally pacing up and down the passageway, chain smoking away his profits from his shop. I tried to calm him down and reassure him. Either he was worried that the adjournment would not be granted or that the agony of his situation would be exposed to all and sundry in the town once this got out – and rest assured it would do. Although the press was not allowed at the proceedings, gossip would find its natural outlet. Being a newsagent and tobacconist meant that most of his customers were men and he felt that he would be a laughing stock. Sneaky asides would be made.

The usher called his name and we followed him through the doors into a vast cathedral-like chamber with a very high ceiling. Masses of dark polished wood were everywhere and high up at the end a dais sat nine men, all looking imposing and severe.

From a distance it seemed, came a voice, "Are you Mr. Bartholomew, case number 24284?"

My client looking very small, whispered, "I am, sir."

The stentorian, disembodied voice said, "Speak up man, the Commissioners wish to hear you."

My client was on the verge of collapse.

I took over, shouting, "Mr. Bartholomew is the taxpayer and I am Mr. St. John, representing him."

The booming voice came again. "There is no need to shout, young man. The Commissioners are quite capable of hearing you."

I already felt deflated and fiddled with my briefcase to find Mr. Bartholomew's files, which I placed on a convenient lectern that was standing on the highly polished tiled floor. I became contrite.

"I'm sorry, sir."

"Alright then, let me explain; I am the Chairman of the Commissioners and an Inspector of Taxes and will now hear from the inspector dealing with your client's case." Apart from that gentleman and the commissioners, I did not realise that there were any other people in the hall.

Suddenly a person, quite near me, seemed to rise and address those on the dais. He informed the men in judgment that tax assessments had been issued and an appeal lodged. No further correspondence or contact had been received from my client, as such he wished the tax assessments to be confirmed, which incidentally was far and above that which my client could pay and was used as a device by the Inland Revenue to force taxpayers to come to heal. He then sat down.

The booming voice asked the Inspector whether he would oppose any adjournment, which apparently he said he would.

This was tricky! Would my bombshell force the gentlemen into traumatic shock and grant my request in a haze of vapours, or worst still, call both of us liars and have us bodily thrown out of the building.

A dilemma was looming and I plunged in. "The request for the adjournment, sirs, is on the basis that my client has suffered a severe shock and could not face the fact that he had to submit his accounts to the Inland Revenue."

The booming voice again, "Shock. What shock? Has he had an accident, been in the hospital or what?"

"Well," I started tentatively. "My client's wife had left him for another woman, sirs," I said subserviently, the word 'sirs' being emphasised. Whatever kudos I could get for being obsequious was welcome.

"Another woman? That's ridiculous," came the retort.

"I assure you, sirs, that this is the truth. My client was traumatised at the time and is still suffering inner pangs."

"So what?" came the voice. "Friendships are forged amongst many people. That is therefore no excuse for your client's behaviour."

I rustled some papers. "I appreciate that, sir, but in this case…" I hesitated, "This is a lesbian relationship."

The voice raised a semi tone. "Preposterous! no such thing."

"I assure you, sirs, that these relationships do happen and unfortunately it happened to my client." I felt the whole excuse to be struck out there and then.

The voice came back to me. "Is that all that you have as an excuse for the failure of your client to comply with the orders of the Tax Acts?"

"Unfortunately yes, sir," I replied – my client looking at me with pleading.

"I don't think it will be accepted," Mr. Bartholomew whispered to me with a certain panic. I gave him a reassuring look, which wasn't much.

The voice came back, "You did say…" he paused "Harrumph, lesbian?" This word was almost whispered. He continued, "The Commissioners will now retire for a short while to consider your request."

With that, all the gentlemen left the platform and went through a side door. I looked at the inspector that opposed our application. He seemed not to want to look at me and kept his head down. At one point he covered his face with his handkerchief, but I am sure I saw his shoulder rocking. Whether in disbelief or by laughing I could not tell, for no sound came from him. Both my client and I sat together not saying a word, praying that I had not caused a furour amongst those distinguished gentlemen; he feeling the pain more, now that it was in the open.

The door opened and the men trooped back to their positions. I tried to detect any sign from them – the same as prisoners in the dock feel waiting for a verdict from the jury.

Suddenly the chairman looked down at me and there was a glimmer of a smile around his lips. All of a sudden his face took on a benign look as he addressed me.

"Mr. St. John," he commenced. "The commissioners have considered your request and they are unanimous in their opinion that what you have told us today, in the annals of excuses, must be the zenith. We have heard in our time reasons for adjournments, ranging from the old chestnut that grandmothers have died, that people have fallen off bicycles, that trains are always late, and that fires had unexpectantly broken out. But yours Mr. St. John, takes the biscuit. Lesbian affair, by God, that is a good one! As such, for your impudence and we must say gentle age, we will grant the adjournment for thirty days. However, we must warn you that if you appear before us again, we will listen very carefully and expect, and may require, a more truthful and respectable reason.

"Note this advice young man, very carefully, for we are sure that you will in the course of your profession, have to attend further meetings of this kind, so think carefully before you utter any more ridiculous excuses on behalf of your clients. If you do, make them as truthful as you can, and as a passing thought, 'acceptable'." With that he dismissed us.

I was tempted to plead that our excuse was genuine. I did not wish to leave the gentlemen with the thought that what I had said was made up. However, my better judgment prevailed and I ushered my client away and rushed from the hall with as much decorum as we could muster. The inspector dealing with the case looked at me in amazement and began shaking his head in disbelief.

Outside the town hall we got into my client's car. Incidentally, you could park your car anywhere it was possible without restriction. Without a word, he then drove me to the station. Before I got out he gave me his records and some money and we shook hands.

I said to him, "Well, we got the adjournment and I'll get cracking on your records. What are you going to do now?"

He looked at me, and for the first time since I had known him, he smiled and said, "I shall do what my wife did and go and live with a woman." With that he drove away, and I am positive that if he would have been on the pavement he would have given a little jig[*].

---

[*] Irish dance

Chapter 8

SALAD DAYS

A friend of theirs who was already a client introduced Elsie and Joe Barton to me. They arrived on the appointed day and time and introduced themselves. Elsie was reasonably broad in size, and short. However, she had a most pleasing bright face and by the sound of her, she was born and bred in the East End of London. Her cockney accent was reasonably pronounced and she epitomised the area and era of her time. She seemed strong-willed and walked in first to my office, pulling her husband behind her, sat down and beckoned him to do the same. Joe Barton was also short and broad like his wife, but against her his bulk seemed normal. He had a small receding chin and a slightly baldish head, which showed when he removed his cap. He looked sheepish and I was sure that during our interview his input would be minimal. Elsie dominated him and it showed. His hands were limp when I shook them and he looked down at his boots without glancing at me.

"Well Mr. and Mrs. Barton, I'm here to help. What is your problem?" I asked both of them, trying to get some response from Joe. He did not answer, but glanced at his wife for some guidance.

She immediately delved into a voluminous shopping bag by her feet, and produced a letter without a word, and handed it to me. There was a sense of defiance about her.

"We've just got this in the post, Mr. St. John, and I don't like it."

The letter that she passed to me requested that a meeting be arranged with the local Inspector of Taxes. There was no hint in the letter as to the reason, just a request for an interview.

"We're only hard working people," she said. "Why do the buggers want to meet us? We've done nothing wrong."

I read the letter again. There was nothing mentioned of anything untoward, nevertheless when a letter is received from the Inland Revenue requesting a meeting, it usually implies that they are not satisfied that the taxpayer's tax returns are correct.

"I don't know why myself," I answered, "so what I propose to do is to telephone the inspector whilst you are here and see if I can gain a reason for the visit."

The conversation that I had with the inspector in question did not throw much light on the visit, except to say, which I already knew, that the Inland Revenue were not satisfied with my clients tax returns. However, he did hint that I look carefully at their savings and the interest on them that they had received. This at least, was a starting point, so I asked Mr. and Mrs. Barton whether they had any savings.

"Of course we have," Elsie answered. "We keep our money in cash or in the Post Office."

In those days, most people did not seem to trust banks for some reason. Savings were either kept under the veritable mattress or in the Post Office. For most working people this form of savings was most convenient. As long as you had a savings account with the Post Office, it was handy to go regularly to deposit monies and withdraw cash without too much fuss.

Apart from that, most folks felt that a bank account would be a hassle, particularly when it came to writing cheques. Unless you were in business, very few individuals would accept cheques, it took days to clear and cash was not instant. Banks made charges and gave very little interest on balances and as such savings were, in theory, depleted. Therefore the Post Office – either as an account or as savings certificates – were giving a better rate of return, and furthermore they were controlled by the government and was more secure. They were solid. In everyone's mind there was no 'jiggery-pokery' with them. Shareholders did not have to be satisfied and financial security with savings was paramount. Further, not that many people could sign their names with the aplomb that those in business could, and therefore it was embarrassing to be requested to do so.

"When can I see the Post Office book then?" I asked, and with a flourish, Elsie dived into the bag again and produced three books, slamming them on my desk.

"There you are then, that's all we have." The belligerent tone came again. I looked at the books and noticed that there was one in the name of Elsie, one in the name of Joe and the third in joint names.

"Why three books?" I asked.

"Well it's as plain as the nose on your face," she answered, as if talking to an imbecile. "I got one for myself, naturally, one for him, of course and one for both of us."

"I can see that," I stated with an air of understanding. I pondered my next question carefully. "Hmmm. Mrs. Barton, can I ask you a personal question?" She gave me a withering look.

"Go on then." I hesitated.

"Mrs. Barton, do you know how much Joe has in his book, and does Joe know what you have?"

"What a bloody silly question to ask. Of course, we know." I felt relieved.

"Don't take offence, Mr. Barton," I said benignly. "But in my experience husbands and wives like to keep their savings quiet from each other." Elsie looked at me aghast.

"Get away," she retorted. "There's no secret between Joe and me. He just leaves all that to me."

"Then why have separate books?" I asked tentatively.

"So we know who's saving the most," she answered with certain logic.

This seemed an interesting competition.

"So," I mentioned. "Why have a joint book?"

"Ah," she answered with a slight smile. "That's from our wages." This reply took time for it so sink in with me.

"So, Mrs. Barton. Where do your savings and those for Joe come from if the joint book is for your wages?"

"Oh that's easy." She seemed more relaxed now. "I work in a canteen factory and sometimes the manager orders too much and what's left over we sell and split the money. Like butter, eggs, cheese and such." This reply seemed perfectly logical to her.

"To be blunt Mrs. Barton," I tentatively said, "It looks like you have been, shall we say, helping yourself in connivance with your manager to the firm's goods."

Elsie stood up to her full five feet, put her hands on my desk and looked directly at me. I shivered somewhat, in front of this harridan of a woman.

"Are you calling me a tealeaf[*]?" I stammered something incoherently. She continued. "This is my living, our future. We're not going to work for the rest of our lives just to receive a brass clock and be put out on our ears when they think we should pack it in."

I could not argue with that. She continued, "This is our right – we do have some pride," she countered.

"And Mr. Barton?" I asked, but was fearful of the reply.

"Oh, him, he's a lorry driver in Covent Garden[†] and what he does, if for instance, he's delivering twenty-five cases of tomatoes, he takes one from each case and ends up with twenty-five tomatoes to sell. Now who's going to notice that one tomato has gone from the box. We're careful, you know."

With that she gave me a sly look. Good job he's not delivering gas cookers. One missing would definitely be noticed, I thought.

"Do both of you do that all the time?" I asked tentatively.

"Of course, how you expect us to make a living?" Presumably there was some form of sense in that answer. "It's not the thieving. No one notices a few bits and pieces missing. Cor blimey! [‡] Everyone's doing it. I bet some of your pencils and envelopes go out the front door. Do you notice? And if you did, what would you do?"

I had an immediate answer to that one. Frankly I had not given it a thought. It made me think for a moment, but then I immediately dismissed the idea. My staff was loyal, upstanding and trustworthy. However, Elsie had planted a distinct doubt in my mind. No, it couldn't happen, as I subconsciously counted the paperclips, which sat in a jar on my desk. How much could

---

[*] English rhyming slag 'Tealeaf' = Thief
[†] Old wholesale fruit market
[‡] Abbreviation for 'cockney slang'. Cor blimey = Blind me

one get for twenty-five paperclips or ten envelopes or fifteen pencils? I tried to banish the thought from my head, but it unfortunately lingered and I made up my mind to do a stock take of the office as soon as possible. But then, wait a moment, time spent on counting the minutia of my office premises could be better spent in earning money, so I immediately dismissed the thought.

"Well let's start by asking some questions, shall we?" I became professional. "Let me ask you then, have you any kids? Do you own your house? Have you a car? Any insurance or endowments? And what about clothes and holidays?"

Elsie looked at Joe and then me and answered emphatically. "No."

"Alright then, how much do you spend on food each week?" Elsie laughed for the first time.

"Are you kidding mate?" I realised then that what she had told me had not really registered.

"I'm sorry, but I've got to ask. I have to build up some picture of your lives. Incidentally, how much does each of you earn?" She gave me a figure for each. Just then, for the first time, Joe spoke up. I had almost forgotten that he was still sitting in front of me.

"Darlin', I earn a little less than you said, I'm sorry." Joe looking sheepish looked down at his boots again.

"Oh yea, that's right," she said and gave me the corrected figure.

"All right, Mr. and Mrs. Barton, I have most of what I need and shall keep these books for a short while."

"Why?"

"I've got to see how much you have saved over the years and if the interest that you have received has gone up appreciably." She looked at me in bewilderment.

"What does that mean?"

"Well, Mrs. Barton, if the interest you have received has gone up a lot, that may be the reason the Inland Revenue wants to see you, because it shows you have saved a lot more money than you should have," I answered.

"But we have," she said. "We put away as much as we can," she continued. "We save all our wages."

"Well, we'll wait and see, shall we?" I counselled.

"But I must have the books in case we want to put more money away," she replied.

"Put it under the mattress for the time being," I said jokingly, and with that they reluctantly left.

I duly met my clients at the offices of the Inland Revenue just prior to the meeting, for which purpose Elsie had put on her best hat with an enormous feather, which I tried to avoid at every occasion she shook her head. Even Joe had changed his cap. However, this was smaller than the one he wore at our interview, and was probably bought many years previously and kept for special occasions such as weddings and funerals. His boots were highly polished and seemed to be pinching his feet, and were most likely bought at the same time as his cap. I warned them to say as little as possible and leave it all to me. I must admit that I had no plan.

I warned Elsie and Joe not to mention how they accumulated their funds, to only answer 'yes' or 'no' on my instructions to any questions, not to elaborate, and to listen carefully to me and my prompts. I knew that really the case was a lost cause. We dare not mention the way the cash had accumulated, as it would put them in an invidious position. To bluff it out was the only solution. I knew that the outcome was going to eventually be additional taxes and probably added interest. My function was to minimise the sum. When Elsie asked me what the result might be before the meeting, I told her my feelings, she blew the roof off.

"More taxes?" she screamed, and when I nodded she went spare* and threatened to walk away. I had to cajole her.

Joe said, "Never mind, Elsie, we can always get more money to pay the taxes," she exploded and told him to shut his mouth. With that, we met the inspector.

The inspector introduced himself to us and stated that he had reason to call the meeting, and as he hinted to me, to discuss the increase in interest from the Post Office savings that the Bartons had enjoyed. He felt that this reflected large sums of monies being deposited and I gave him the Post Office accounts to investigate. He took each year separately for three years and added up the net deposits and compared the amounts with the salaries that the Bartons earned. Of course, as I found out myself, there were discrepancies each year. More monies had been saved than the salaries already declared.

A point picked by the Inspector, and one that I had already noticed, was that the salaries that the Bartons earned was similar to their deposits in the joint account, which at my interview with them in my office confirmed that they had told me.

The inspector then asked the questions that I had already asked Elsie about living expenses, etc. I endeavoured to marry these with the income enjoyed by the Bartons, and naturally came to the same conclusion, which engendered their reply as to the canteen and Covent Garden.

---

* Going crazy

I will say that during the interview, Elsie gave the Inland Revenue the monosyllabic answers I had instructed her to. I will give her her due, the answers she gave were not through misunderstanding the questions, but because she was a wily individual and understood full well the position she and Joe were in. Every time Joe wished to say anything, he got a withering look from his wife and closed his mouth quietly.

The inspector persisted with his questioning and was getting nowhere, and frustration was creeping in. A long hour passed without success or reaching a conclusion; Elsie sat passively, although seething inside and Joe was already, in his mind, at another place. I could see that the meeting was going nowhere as far as the Inland Revenue were concerned, and I could see no way out of the impasse that the questioning was taking. I was trying desperately to find a solution satisfactory to both sides, but it was frustrating. The circles we were going round was making dizziness a top priority, and I felt that under such circumstances, the Inland Revenue, with their vast resources of wealth should at least have supplied sick bags. Suddenly though, salvation loomed for my clients, through inspiration on my part, when the inspector, in his frustration, spoke these immortal words.

"I think that the accumulation in your wealth Mr. and Mrs. Barton came from theft."

Eureka! That was it! My lifeline. I acted immediately with shock and horror. I told the Bartons to get up as we were leaving immediately, that the meeting was terminated, and that the inspector had exceeded his authority, that my clients had been grossly insulted and finally that come 'Hell or High Water', I would not deal with this particular inspector.

He looked at me in astonishment as I ushered the Bartons quickly out of the room. This was difficult because as I informed you previously, Elsie was rotund. Nevertheless, with Joe trailing behind, it was achieved. I put my fingers to my lips to indicate silence until we had left the building. Outside, the bewildered pair looked at me quizzically.

"Why did you do that, Mr. St. John?" Elsie asked. I tried to explain as best I could, that it was solely a ploy to get them out of a no-win situation. Elsie was aghast.

"But it's the truth," she said. "We were nicking the stuff and selling it."

I tried again to explain. "I know that, and you know that, but the inspector had no right to bring it up. As far as I'm concerned, it was an insult to your integrity." Both the partners looked at me in bewilderment, but it was impossible to explain to them the subtle nuances involved. I said, "You have your Post Office books back, and I will be in touch with you. That is, if I hear any further from them."

With that, we parted on the pavement with Elsie dragging Joe away, both shaking their heads in a daze.

Almost a year had passed and I gave no particular thought to the Barton's case, until one day a district inspector from the office we had visited contacted me. Now a district inspector as the name implies, is the boss, big cheese, top honcho in the area – well above the rank of the inspector level that we had met. He wanted to know whether we could have a chat in his office between ourselves, and without my clients being present. Of course I accepted his request, and on the appointed day and time presented myself to him.

He was affable in his greeting towards me and after the customary discussion on the weather forecast and the state of English sport, he spoke, "I note from my file on Mr. and Mrs. Barton, that you had a meeting with one of my inspectors and that suddenly you upped and left with your clients. Why?"

This is where I had to bluff this out. Crunch time!

"It would seem that your associate insulted my clients," I said, throwing the ball into his court.

The inspector gave me a sharp look and said, "How so?"

"He called my clients thieves."

"He did what?" There was an incredulous look on his face. I decided to give him a superior stare, but I also did not wish to alienate my position with the Revenue – I tried to be conciliatory.

"I don't suppose he meant it, nevertheless he did say it and I felt that my only action would be to terminate the meeting immediately."

The inspector nodded and looked down at the file on his desk. "Quite so," he said. "I don't suppose you had any alternative. I would have felt that you might have remonstrated with him and kept the interview going." His pleading look to me when he said that would in normal circumstances have moved me, but my clients were in a precarious position and it was incumbent upon me to fight their corner.

I said, "I could have done without taking umbrage, but I felt that your colleague, by his questioning, which was fairly long and in depth, was getting nowhere and as such it seemed to me that he was frustrated and unfortunately his frustration came to the fore."

The inspector put his fingers together in some form of prayer and said pleadingly, "Can we not forget the incident and discuss the case as man to man? I don't want this walk out to affect my chap's career." He looked at me with the wish that I would not take this to higher authority. Got you, I thought!

"Now I don't want to blot his copy book with your superiors. So if you and I could settle this case over this desk, naturally without penalties and interest, I'm sure that I could

111

convince my clients to settle any tax liability we can agree is due and close the file."

I looked at the inspector expectantly and the inspector looked at me and said, "That sounds reasonable to me. So let's get down to a figure we can agree on."

Some figures were then bandied about and eventually a suitable figure was agreed upon, which I thought was an ideal figure for my clients.

I said to the Inspector, "I shall naturally present your figure to my clients, as I need their approval, but I can assure you that I will recommend it."

After various pleasantries, I left to contact Elsie and Joe. When I eventually told them the result they reluctantly agreed and parted with the words, "Instead of one tomato, for the next few months it will have to be two."

Chapter 9

FILES, FILES AND MORE FILES

Prior to the curse and atrocity of computers, all professional and businesses had files. No, dummy! Not for your nails, but for holding papers, documents, accounts, working papers, etc. Files were an essential part of business, something that they could not do without. The loss of a file was catastrophic. I could never understand the term 'pocket file', you could not, in the wildest stretch of your imagination, put one in your pocket. Therefore, usually files were a folded piece of cardboard and papers were attached with tags. I had to eventually purchase twenty filing cabinets, although most were empty, as the bulk of the files were strewn throughout my office. But the cabinets had to be purchased to hold the monstrosities. Each file was headed by marking pen with the name of the client and a number. Now I have always had a fascination when I received a letter from another accountant or solicitor, to look at the reference number shown at the top of their letter. That would usually roughly indicate the amount of clients that they were dealing with. Therefore, to show that my practice was larger than it was I would use the following references for example. Fortheringay was F10, Floulkes-French was F20 and Frankenstein F30, and so on. Thus if I wrote a letter for Frankenstein, anyone looking at the reference would assume that I had thirty clients with the initial 'F', instead of the three I already had. Clever, eh?

The Inland Revenue, also naturally used files of a buff colour and these were numbered but not initialised. Therefore, with the amount of taxpayers who were self-employed the numbers reached astronomical proportions. Even to this day, the numbers on the files that they hold have a ten-figure number, supplemented now with a National Insurance* Number. To write to them curtails quoting a sixteen figure number interspersed with three capital letters. Heaven forbid that a number or initial is incorrectly entered – confusion would reign supreme. Secretaries who write letters on your behalf spend most of their time typing in so many numbers and initials that as bosses we are paying for how long the references are typed, which can take up to a quarter of the time. Banks are no better as they use sort codes of six numbers and to accompany that for the accounts of their clients they use eight numbers to distinguish the bank account. Building societies can collapse under thirteen numbers. By the time you have telephoned any of these institutions, and quoted the reference number – invariably having to repeat it – you have forgotten the question you wanted to ask. In the meantime, your telephone bill is rising. and then, either they cannot trace the file or the person dealing with it is out at lunch; your telephone bill becomes abortive.

All this brings me neatly to the case of my client, Ted Andrews. Now Ted owned a modest shop in the high street, selling an unusual and specialised product for a particular hobby. All his customers were avid and excited by their pursuits. They would spend ages in the shop over their particular purchase and although Ted was an expert in his field, questions were thrown at him that occasionally flummoxed him, but he would always try to find a suitable answer. To Ted, his

---

* Social security

business was also his personal hobby. He would chat for hours with his customers and his enthusiasm would shine through. Because of Ted's attitude to the business and the time spent chin wagging*, sales were not spectacular. Ted did not care. Business was secondary to his desires. It was an adjunct to the hobby he pursued and loved. He could not wait to open the shop so that he could talk, and advise his customers. He even carried on during closing time, and with telephone questions. Weekends were used to pursue his hobby and to all intents it was a man's game. Very few women were involved and that suited Ted fine, as he was a confirmed bachelor and wifely duties he felt, would encroach on his pastime. He was content. Seasons came and went and passed him by. The shop became a meeting place for fellow lovers of the sport.

Unfortunately, his lack of adequate sales over a number of years came to the attention of the Inland Revenue, who started a correspondence with me. I say started, but in fact I was bombarded, for the first letter I received from them consisted of three pages of foolscap paper, every inch of which was covered by questions. This was, by far, the longest opening letter from them that I had so far received and needed considerable amount of work and research to reply. I informed Ted immediately of the receipt and arranged a meeting with him, to go over it and reply to their inquiries.

When I met Ted to answer the letter, a thought struck me upon reading it again, that it was not only nitpicking, but also very intrusive. I thought it best to just answer the questions posed with a simple 'yes' or 'no' if possible and not go too much into details and see the response. The reply was, even by the Inland Revenue standards, exceptional. I received a four-page foolscap letter, even more detailed than the first – not only going over the same ground, adding further inquiries of even a more intrusive nature. This was now going into the realms of

---

* Small talk

absurd. I met Ted again and we replied as best we could, although there was no hint in the letter as to the sex of the writer; in my biased way, and by the tone of the questions, I came to the conclusion that the inspector dealing with my client was a woman, and Ted was going to be the stepping stone for her advancement in the department. The Inland Revenue was male dominated in senior positions at the time and this particular inspector had to make her mark against her colleagues. With such bias as I had, downfall soon followed.

We answered as best as we could and thought wrongly that was the end of the matter. Surely they were now satisfied and could leave me and particularly Ted in peace. But no! Another missive arrived, just as long as previously and as probing.

"Damn and blast their eyes," I thought. I could see that I would have to give up seeing to my clients solely to spend my time replying to the Inland Revenue, and that Ted would have to discard his hobby, which he dearly loved, to deal with this manic inspector. I felt that we could not take this any further as it started to ruin my practice and Ted's life. The only way out of this impasse was to see a) the inspector or b) try and find out what he was really after in a telephone call. Thus I chose the latter and telephoned their office, to be put through to the individual. He answered, and I was already in a quandary. The voice was effeminate, but I could detect a male countenance. I could not ask the first name of he/she, as that would not be allowed. I could not request a photograph to see whether my correspondent was a cross-dresser. All I could hope for, that in our conversation, a hint of a pipe being placed down or at least hearing a moustache bristle – to no avail.

When I broached the subject of my client and the copious correspondence we had received, he/she was adamant that they had to reach the truth. In a minor way, that is what I was after as to the sex of this individual. I asked this person how far this was going and got an annoyed response. I felt he/she was stamping his/her foot. This was not good. Our conversation ended without any hint or result. This rarely happened; usually between accountants and the Inland Revenue was a certain, unwritten law that a hint of any problem would be dropped in the conversation. Cooperation between were implied – not freely given, but subtly dropped in the course of talks.

With this inspector such niceties were abandoned and I began to be frustrated. I waited for the next missive from this person with certain trepidation. I did not have to wait long to receive another 'book' of questions and implications. Now I was getting annoyed. I saw Ted and told him that I felt I should speak to his/her superior, but warned him of the consequences. My idea could open a 'Pandora's Box' if I approached the District Inspector (who was head of the area) and he/she's boss. They could close ranks, which could be detrimental to my client. Ted said I should go for it. He was also frustrated with the shenanigans of the Inland Revenue and wanted to concentrate on his shop.

This was affecting him severely and he was feeling that the whole situation was getting out of hand. I therefore waited before I approached the District Inspector, weighing up the results that could come from my actions. Luck was with us, did I but know it.

A few days later, Ted rang me and he sounded upset and disturbed. "Mr. St. John, don't you want me as a client anymore?" I thought that this opening gambit was characteristic of him.

"Of course, Mr. Andrews I want you. Why do you ask?"

"Well, "you've returned my file to me."

This was a surprise and I asked, "What file?"

"I've just opened a parcel and inside was a file with my name on it." I felt a tingle down my back and the hairs on the back of my head stood up. I clutched at straws.

"Mr. Andrews. What colour is the file and is there a number on it?" I kept my fingers and everything else crossed, waiting expectantly for his reply.

"Mr. St. John, it is brown and yes there is a number on it," Eureka!

"Keep the file safe, Mr. Andrews, very safe, and I am sending a car to you to collect the file. Mr. Andrews, say nothing to anyone. Repack the file in non-see through paper, make sure the driver signs for it and mark the parcel for my sole and private attention. This may be our salvation."

I don't think he understood the implications of what I was saying, but I sent the car to him post haste, and on its return to me with the parcel I saw the file. In my excitement I over tipped the driver and almost hugged him. The file was as I suspected, my client's file held by the Inland Revenue. This incident made me remember that many years previously, a colleague was involved in a serious case with the Inland Revenue and his client, and considerable sums were involved in back taxes. The client's file turned up at my colleague's offices, and the Inland Revenue, being informed of that fact, had to drop their case in the belief that the accountant had read the file, and seen all the arguments that they had, and all the information that was held; as such their case against his client was compromised. This memory came back to me. I must admit that when my colleague told me of that incident, I was skeptical and felt that he might have embroidered the story. I could not believe that the Inland Revenue could be that stupid or negligent to release a file through the post, but it just happened to us.

It was late in the afternoon when I obtained the file and tossed up in my mind whether I should report this now or wait for the morning. However, I thought if I did it now there would be 'brownie points' to be gained. So I rang the District Inspector confidentially, thereby bypassing the inspector that I was dealing with. I got through.

"Is that the District Inspector, as I only wish to speak to him?" I demanded.

He replied, "Yes I am the District Inspector. Why do you ask?"

"It would seem that a terrible, and I emphasise terrible, mistake has been made by your office." He was hesitant.

"Such as?"

"For some reason my client has received his file from your office," I said this deferentially, but with a slight smirk.

"Good God!!! I don't suppose you have read it, have you?" He sounded frustrated, annoyed, apprehensive and somewhat servile.

"Of course not," I lied and said. "Can we make an appointment for tomorrow to return the file to you, and frankly, it must only be handed to you personally, as we do not wish for this to be spread among your staff?"

"That's very kind of you, Mr. St. John, I will look forward to seeing you on a personal basis; man to man, so to speak."

A time was mentioned and I duly arrived at his office with the file under my arm, covered in brown unmarked paper, as if it was a pornographic missive.

In the Civil Service, in the old days, your office position and fixtures measured progress. It was a bizarre situation, that the more authority you reached, the more you obtained in accoutrements. For instance, you would start sharing offices with others, then progress to your own office with bare essentials, and then your rise through the ranks would be accompanied by windows, carpeting and hat stands. When you

119

visited the Inland Revenue, his office and fixtures would show the status of the inspector in the hierarchy. A District Inspector would therefore have a single office with two windows, fitted carpet and the veritable hat stand. You were then in the presence of a government mandarin. All these items were present in the office, except that he had three windows. Heavens to Murgatroyd! He was high up in the service.

I was quite impressed as he greeted me almost like a lost brother, shook my hand warmly, and ushered me to a chair in front of his desk.

"Are you comfortable, Mr. St. John? Do you want a cigarette? Coffee or tea?" I had never been treated by a government department like this previously and thought I should milk the situation for all it's worth, as I will not be treated like this again in the future. So I accepted the cigarette, the coffee and when this arrived there was even biscuits available. This was something to put in my diary. At least I could see where some of my taxes were being judicially spent. It was not being thrown away on the military, plush government offices and perks for the boys.

"Thank you, Mr. St. John for your prompt return of the file." He definitely looked relieved as he stirred his tea with a spoon.

I will say that the District Inspector was a charmer. I suppose that was why he was head of the department. He ignored the file for a moment and concentrated on frivolities, state of the weather, traffic, English football and rugby, the usual guff, trying to relax me before he questioned me over the file and my client. I knew the procedure well and played along with the game, biding my time. Then Mr. Clinton began his opening gambit.

"Mr. St. John, you told me that you have not read the file. Is that correct?" I demurred.

"Frankly Mr. Clinton, strictly speaking, I did not read the file, but I had to be sure that it was my client's file in the Inland Revenue." I put on an innocent face.

He looked at me over his glasses and said "Quite. Quite. You had to be sure, didn't you?" I nodded, enjoying the game we were playing.

"I must admit however, that your inspector was being obstreperous with me and my client, and his correspondence to me over such a small inquiry far exceeded his power in my opinion." The Inspector opened my client's file before him.

"Yes, I see what you mean," he said, studying the correspondence. He looked at me with a concentrated stare. "Did you find that the letters you received from us were somewhat peculiar?" he asked.

I did not want to get involved with the gender of the inspector that I dealt with, and said, "I must say that the tone and volume of the letters was excessive to the extreme." The inspector nodded.

"Unfortunately, this is not the first case I have looked at being dealt with by that gentleman," he emphasised the word 'gentleman'. He continued, "I've had to try and curb his enthusiasm and point out that although we have a difficult job, we do also have to have some compassion to the taxpayer." I nodded sagely at this remark. He continued, "I'm trying desperately to get this gentleman," again the emphasis on the word 'gentleman', "Transferred to another district, preferably in the Outer Hebrides*, as he is upsetting the other staff in my district and is causing chaos and a headache to me." With this remark, he smiled. "However, tell me about your Client?"

I went into a long summary of Mr. Ted Andrews' trading, his hobby, passion for the business, and his desire to continue

---

* Islands in remote part of Scotland

to concentrate on his sport and that of his customers. I laid it on thick and pointed out that Mr. Andrews was a paragon of virtue, which if the truth be told he was.

The inspector nodded now and then during my discourse and eventually said to me, "From what you have told me, Mr. St. John, and the fact that your client received his file, I feel that we can say from our perspective, the enquiries into your client's affairs are now closed." With that he closed the file and looked at me and smiled.

"Mr. Clinton," I said, looking directly at him, "Can you please let me have confirmation of that remark? Can you also please let me know how my client's file was sent to him?"

The Inspector glowered at me. "I can tell you in no uncertain terms," he said. "We in the Inland Revenue, have to apply for Head Office for every damn thing we need. If I require paperclips, I have to have a bloody good excuse for wanting them. I applied three months ago for a pair of scissors and I have still not gotten them." His face took on a crimson hue. "Every bloody thing we want has to be supplied for and vetted by some fool Civil Servant in headquarters at the Treasury and it is up to some pip-squeak to approve it."

He threw his hands in the air in exasperation and continued. "I suppose you noticed when you came to my office that below me is the Department of Employment. Now they have everything, paperclips, scissors, and more importantly a van, which they use to carry files from office to office. Damn their eyes, they even have plants throughout their offices. Whatever the buggers want they immediately get." He was now getting angry and warming to his theme.

"We get the money from the taxpayer and they spend it." I had never seen an inspector so animated. "I think we should, in this office, have a shoot in the corner going down to them and all we have to do is put the money we received in taxes down the shoot for them to spend." With that he looked at the heavens.

"As I said, they have a van to transfer files and we have to send them by post, as it's cheaper." He was banging his desk with fervour. "That's why your client got the file, through some cock-up in the office. Why can't we have a van?" He was pleading to me now. "We transfer more files than the bastards downstairs. Their van and driver sit in the courtyard for days on end doing nothing. I even wish I had his job." He got up and looked out the window. "Come, Mr. St. John and look down and you'll see the bloody van just sitting there."

I got up and went to the window and saw the van parked and the driver standing next to it, reading a newspaper and drinking coffee from a mug.

"See, Mr. St. John, I'm not lying am I?" He was glum and returned to his desk. I felt it not prudent to pass my opinion during the inspector's diatribe against his own department and that of those below him. I then thought to get into his good books it would be wise to take sides with him, as he was getting more distraught over his job, department and the Civil Service in general.

"Nevertheless, Mr. Clinton, you are basically happy with your work, aren't you?" He gave me a searching look.

"Mr. St. John, I have been in this department for many years and have reached my exalted position," he said with a certain pique. "I have studied and smoothed up those I felt would help me in my career, and I am now disillusioned with the whole thing, but I am stuck with it; roll on my retirement, which I am sure I will spend in your client's shop and thoroughly enjoy it".

All I could do was tut-tut to his final remarks and after further frivolities I left his office, with him looking downcast. I was sure that he went back to the window and looked down at the van with a certain longing.

When I left the building, I went directly to Ted's shop and told him the good news. All he could say was that he was relieved and hoped that he could continue with his sport without any further interruptions from government departments, and to leave him to carry on with his hobby. I gave him further good news that in a short time he would get a new customer in the shape of the inspector.

Chapter 10

RAGS TO RICHES

Eddy Cochrane was a cockney. He came from a long line of cockneys, whose patch was the East End of London. His antecedents were 'duckers and divers', 'twisters and turners', people that could turn a penny quite quickly. They could buy and sell anything and everything, whether it be tied down or not. Life gave them the opportunity to see the profit in most things. They could also see the advantage of dealing. Whatever the product, there was money to be made. His family had been what was then known as 'rag and bone' people. In the nineteenth-century, rags were sold and bought to make clothes for the poor. The bones were bought and sold from farms to butchers and the public to make soup for poor families. They were the veritable 'Steptoes'* and their genes were implanted in Eddy. With him it became an established business, no costermonging. He had a yard surrounded by fencing on top of which was barbed wire and an Alsatian dog roaming the yard as security to ward off any undesirables – a loveable animal when he was with his master, but woe betide any intruder. He would put his fangs in their arm or leg and thus they were caught. He had the instincts of a police dog without the discipline or

---

* TV programme comedy on second-hand dealers

training. He did slobber over me when I visited, and I thought that I had psychologically tamed him, but Eddy was always in the background, which disillusioned me in my power with animals. During my meetings with the dog he was always glancing towards his master, who was putting his fingers to his lips to quiet the animal.

Eddy had a scrapyard, which housed anything and everything.

Most of the items were made of some sort of metal from old bed-sted's[*] to car engines, and old pots and pans. Whatever was not sold to customers was sent to the smelters for converting into raw metals, and sold. As such, the business thrived sufficiently to give Eddie a reasonable income for him to support his wife, three kids and a mortgage in a moderate terraced house in the area. Some weeks his income was reasonable and others next to nothing. It was a precarious living; nevertheless Eddy enjoyed the cut and thrust of his trading and could indulge in his one and only pastime, and that was pony trotting. For this he had a pony and trap, both of which he kept in a local stable yard. He would spend his spare time – with the help of his children – brushing down the animal, feeding it and polishing the brass and leather straps of the trap. This consisted of a single seat attached to two wheels and a harness for the pony, solely for this unusual sport. It could not conceivably be used for family outings, as the trap was too small.

On visits to the track, the pony would go into a borrowed horsebox from the yard; the family would pile in and the trap attached to the back of the horsebox. The whole family was involved and enthusiastic. There was no money to be made from winning. You could, at a pinch, have a bet on the outcome, but you had to be conversant with the sport, and knowledgeable. They were not speed racers, as in normal

---

[*] Iron bed

horse racing, but a skillful sport where the running of the competitors was banned – almost to be compared with walking events at the Olympics where both feet had to be in contact with the road, and where observance to the rules was paramount. The whole sport was unusual to the extreme and riders came from all walks of life, without any class distinction.

Furthermore, apart from feed, travelling and vets bills, the game was reasonably inexpensive – and in Eddy's case was a throw back to the old horse and cart of his predecessors, albeit with a little more finesse.

Then the letter arrived from the Inland Revenue requesting a visit to them by Eddy and me.

"What the bloody hell do they want?" was his initial response. "Cor blimey, I've tried to make a crust and now the swines want to see me." I tried to placate him.

"Don't worry, Eddy, firstly I will be with you and secondly I don't think that they have any grounds for the meeting." I was not confident with that second thought.

Eddy's trading was precarious, furthermore what he traded in could be considered not a legitimate business. The trade had elements of nefarious dealings, which smelled of bias in the eyes of the Inland Revenue. So much could be hidden as most sales were in cash; there was a feeling that there could be room for tax evasion.* Stock in trade was fairly fluid in valuation and therefore changed up or down to suit the circumstances. Eddy did keep fairly good records and for every sale or purchase invoices were demanded and given. This was partly for the benefit of the Inland Revenue and also for the police in case certain items dealt with were stolen. Names and addresses were also given and noted, but as far as the Inland Revenue was concerned this could be construed as a 'Mickey

---

* Inventory

127

Mouse' operation that opened many avenues for avoiding the correct tax being payable.

These were my thoughts as I telephoned Mr. Cox, the inspector for the appointment. We agreed on a date and time and I informed Eddy that we would meet there. I gave him three instructions 1) to be monosyllabic in his answers, 2) to take the lead from me, and most importantly, 3) not to lose his temper.

We entered the office and Mr. Cox greeted both of us and ushered us to the chairs in front of his desk. He introduced himself and opened the meeting.

"Mr. Cochrane, I am an Inspector of Taxes and my function is to look into the affairs of certain taxpayers."

At this remark, Eddy jumped up and said, "What the bloody hell do you mean affairs? I've been true to my wife for years and you won't find me knocking off any other woman but her." The inspector looked up to the ceiling in frustration. He'd heard this response so many times when the word 'affair' was mentioned, that he had a stock answer.

"No, Mr. Cochrane," he said with a shrug of his shoulders in resignation. "Not that type of affair. It's a word we use. I mean look into your trading and your means."

Cochrane would not be placated. "Who are you calling mean?" Mr. Cox sighed and probably thought that I have got a right one here.

"You still do not understand. Perhaps Mr. St. John will give you a better explanation," he said, throwing the ball into my court.

"The inspector wants to check on the money you have as profit in the business and how you spend it," I explained.

Eddy looked at me and said, "Why does this geezer want to know how I spend my money?"

Before the interview had started the rules that I had laid down with Eddy not to argue had gone by the board. I knocked him under the desk and gave him a severe look.

I then said to Mr. Cox, "Let's try and ignore your preamble and we will see how we progress. Shall we?" The inspector nodded and looked down at his notes.

"Tell me, Mr. Cochrane, how much do you spend on food each week?"

Eddy ignoring my stare, said, "Food! We all got to eat ain't we?"

"I know that. All I want to know is how much you spend," the inspector said.

"I don't know. I give the missus* money when she wants it and there is always grub† on the table for us," Eddy replied.

"Well how much?" The inspector insisted.

"How the fuck do I know. I give her what she wants and I don't argue. She's a good girl. She won't fuck me." I gave Eddy another kick.

The inspector gave him another severe look and wrote something down. He continued, "How many cars do you own?"

"Cars? What cars? I got a bleeding lorry and that's that." He continued in the same vein. "Even that's due for the knackers yard."

"I appreciate, Mr. Cochrane that you need a lorry in the business, but how do you get to the yard and for shopping and weekends for instance?"

"I told you I've got this banger of a lorry, which I use, and I park it in the road I live in. The missus goes shopping and

---

* Cockney for wife
† Food

takes one of the kids sometimes to help 'er. Who needs the lorry for Sundays?" He was getting angry again and I started kicking him. If he got large bruises it was his fault.

"It's enuff I have to drive the bugger for work."

"So you don't for instance, go to the country at weekends?" The inspector queried.

"Wot you on about?" Eddy said looking directly at Mr. Cox.

"Well a lorry would not be able to go down those country lanes very well. Wouldn't it?"

Eddy looked at me with a questioning stare, as if to ask where this was leading and frankly I did not myself understand.

"Wot do I want to go down country lanes for?" The inspector looked down at his notes again and said, "Well for instance to visit a secluded house."

"Wots that?" Eddy asked.

"A house hidden from view for supposition," Mr. Cox replied.

"Gordon Bennet!" Eddy exclaimed. "Why would I do that?"

"You tell me," the inspector replied. I was flummoxed at this line of questioning. I looked at Eddy and he looked at me. I felt that I had to say something and did.

"I fail to understand this line of questioning. Can you please elaborate?"

"Alright," Cox said. "We understand that your client has a house in the country," Eddy laughed.

"Strewth, you must be kidding."

"No, I'm quite serious," said Mr. Cox and continued, "Do you like boats Mr. Cochrane?"

"I can take 'em or leave 'em. I did once row a boat on the canal, but I lost a bleeding oar. What a fucking mess." Eddy grinned for the first time at the thought. Mr. Cox looked again at his notes.

"Do you own a boat?"

"I think one came into the yard at one time, but it was useless and I cut it up for firewood."

The tenor of the questioning was still puzzling to me, but I felt I was getting the gist and it was spooky. I therefore let it carry on for a little longer, noticing that the inspector was writing feverishly on his pad and glancing again at the file.

"Let me try something else," he continued. "Do you like horse racing?" Eddy was emphatic in his reply.

"No I bloody don't."

"Well most people do," Cox stated. "You know they like a flutter on the Derby* or Grand National."

"Fucked if I do. I got better ways to spend me dosh†," Eddie stated.

"Let me ask you then. Do you own a horse?" Eddy was adamant.

"No." I looked at him and noticed a slight smile hovering on his lips. I knew he was going to be pedantic.

"Come on, Mr. Cochrane. I have it on good authority that you do," Cox said.

---

* Important horse race meetings with national coverage
† Slang for cash money

131

Now we were getting somewhere. The penny dropped. The Inland Revenue has various means of obtaining information on taxpayers. One of which was through anonymous letters. Each one, however bizarre was taken seriously, as some contained a semblance of truth. I was sure that was what Mr. Cox was quoting from and extrapolated his inquiries.

I again gave Eddy a kick under the desk. With all the kicks I had given him, I was sure that when we left the office Eddy would have to be in a wheelchair.

"Wot the bloody 'ell are you on about?" he said, staring at me. I tried to get out of it.

"I'm sorry Eddy, my leg must have had a twitch."

"Behave yourself matey." Eddie admonished me. "Control your bleeding foot."

The inspector looked at Eddy and then me. I kept my head down, pretending to look at my notes.

"I will ask you again, Mr. Cochrane, do you own a horse, or to refresh your memory, did you ever own a horse?"

Eddy stared straight at the inspector and with a deep sigh said, "No, I've never had an 'orse and don't have any 'orses." Mr. Cox gave him a searching look.

"I have it on impeccable information that you do," and with that he flourished from the file a sheet of paper, and triumphantly placed it face up on the desk in front of us.

We could see straight away that it was a copy of a small newspaper advertisement advertising the sale of manure. In bold letters was Eddy's name and address. Eddy took the sheet of paper, tore it into little bits and threw it on the desk, exclaiming "Shit!" Mr. Cox sighed.

"Don't worry, Mr. Cochrane, we have other copies. And I believe that your remark just now, in your vernacular, is the same as the advertisement." Oh! How triumphant and heroic the inspector felt and continued.

"And you say that you don't have a horse or even horses?" Eddy smirked again.

"That's right guvnor, I don't have a 'orse or even 'orses." I knew that Eddy was playing games with Mr. Cox and I wasn't too happy. I must admit, nevertheless, that there was a certain delicious air cropping into the interview.

"Do not play games with me, Mr. Cochrane. Where then do you get the manure to sell, if you don't own horses, or a horse? Do you buy it from outside?" Eddy looked at him.

"I might deal in lots of different things, but shit is not one of them."

The inspector was looking visibly frustrated now. He put on a menacing tone. "I shall ask you for the last time. Listen to me carefully, because a lot depends on your answer. Apart from the advertisement I have shown you, I understand that you own horses for racing and other pursuits and therefore, unless I get a straight answer to my questions, the situation could be very serious." Eddy looked at me carefully and I gave him a slight nod of the head.

"Alright, Mister, I'll come clean. I don't own an 'orse or 'orses as such. I do have a pony. It's not an 'orse as such as you know it. Strictly speaking, it's like a kid and grown up. They're different."

Cox looked at him and sneered. "Why didn't you say so before all these shenanigans?"

"Well you didn't ask about ponies. You asked about 'orses. I don't want an 'orse. I like ponies."

The inspector put his fingers together with a resigned shrug of the shoulders and continued. "Alright, I accept what you consider the difference. However I know that pony lessons for children cost money. How much does it cost you a week to feed, stable and have lessons?" Eddy looked at him in amazement.

"It cost me bugger all. Firstly, I don't allow the kids to ride the nag. Second, I don't ride it, and thirdly the crap I sell pays for its feed."

Cox stared at him. "So why have it?"

"Cos I want it for me 'obby."

"What hobby?"

"Pony trottin."

Cox was now perplexed. "What's that, and how much does it cost?" Eddy stared at him with a surprised look on his face, as if everyone knew what pony trotting was all about – and said as if speaking to a child.

"You don't know? All right, I'll tell ya. I takes the pony to a track and sit on a saddle attached to the reigns of the pony and we trot around against others. We're not allowed to race."

"Alright, I think I understand, but probably don't appreciate the niceties of the sport. But how much does it cost you and what do you win?"

"Sod all," Eddy answered emphatically.

"But it must cost something. Horses, I'm sorry, ponies are not cheap." Eddy sighed as if speaking to an imbecile.

"Look 'ere mate. The shit pays for the nag's food. Me friend takes me in an 'orse box and the family wiv ese. 'Ei's the one that's got the stables. We both 'ave a go. I should be so lucky to win, but if I do, I win a cup. No spondooliks[*]. I've even had the kids saying I should 'ave the cups melted down for loot. I give 'em a clip round the ears for that."

All of a sudden the inspector changed tack to both our surprises. Occasionally in interviews with the Inland Revenue these tactics are used to shock the interviewee to flummox him into admitting something that he is not prepared for, and to catch him off guard.

"Marbella must have been pleasant when you were there," he remarked twiddling with his pen.

"Wots that?" Eddy said in puzzlement.

"Marbella is in Spain," Cox said.

"Christ you learn somfing new every day."

"Don't tell me you have never been to Spain?" The inspector ventured. Eddy looked at him.

"No I bloody 'aven't. Can't abide bloody foreigners." Cox looked at the file again.

"So you're telling me that you have never been abroad?"

"I just told you I don't like foreigners or their rotten food, lingo and their 'abits. And I ain't got a passport," Eddy said triumphantly, like a true Englishman and patriot.

"But most people have, and holidays on the continent are now quite cheap, except of course in Marbella," Cox emphasised the name of the resort.

"Well I bloody well don't and I don't want one." The inspector looked at him in the eye and asked.

"So where do you go for your vacation?"

"Wots that?" Cox shrugged again.

---

[*] A British slang for money

"Your holiday. Where do you go with Mrs. Cochran and your children?"

Eddy chided in "Wots an 'oliday?"

"Come on, Mr. Cochrane, everyone has a holiday during the year."

"Perhaps you do. Sitting in your office and being paid by the likes of me, wiv me taxes. But I can't afford an 'oliday."

"Not even a week's break?"

Cox was not being cynical. This exchange between the two of them was, to my eyes, being handled extremely well by my client and did not require my intervention. Eddy was now on the verge of frustration and said with certain venom.

"I told you once and I'll tell you again, I don't 'ave 'olidays." He emphasised the word 'Holidays'. "If I did, who would feed the dog in the yard? How could I sell anyfing if I was away? Who would muck-out the pony? And where would I get the moolah for such rubbish? Me missus and me kids are 'appy to muck about the kitchen and streets and 'elp me 'obby. That's all they want."

The inspector looked again at the file and asked, "Can you fly, Mr. Cochran?" Eddy looked at me in disbelief.

"Only if I jump orf your bleeding roof with a pair of wings like that greek geezer. Who was it now? I fink 'is name was Icaratis or somefing foreign."

"Icaris," the inspector corrected him.

"Yea that's 'im," Eddy agreed.

It had now reached the stage in the interview where I felt that I had to put my two penny worth and said, "Mr. Cox, I'm following this bizarre interview with more and more wonderment. The questions you are asking my client about houses in the country, horses, holidays on the Costa de Sol, cars, and now flying can only, in my opinion, stem from an anonymous letter that you have and are asking questions, which I consider to be a fishing trip. You can deny it if you wish, but I feel now that no useful purpose will be gained by these manoeuvers. Apart from the advertisement that you have shown us, which I would point out, my client acknowledges, you have no concrete proof of anything you have asked him." With that little speech, Eddy looked at me with a certain admiration, which frankly was not deserved.

Mr. Cox shuffled the papers in the file and his face turned slightly red – only slightly mind you. He was an inspector after all, and very little would phase him. He made a gesture to me.

"I suppose there is no reason why I should not tell you that we have had a letter about your client. I cannot however, confirm or deny whether it was anonymous or not."

Eddy, on that reply, went berserk. "Those bastards in the trotting game are bleeding well annoyed with me. They don't like it 'cos I get up their bloody noses. Them with their 'igh-faluting ideas, don't like the likes of me doing my fing. Some of 'em think I'm beneaf 'em. I'll show the swine's next time I see 'em. Some of 'em are due for a bunch of fives,* mark my words, for putting me frew this and they're going to pay."

I held Eddy's arm and tried to placate him, whilst Mr. Cox looked on in some embarrassment. I then rose to leave and tried to steer Eddy out of the room.

"Now, Eddy lets go. Mr. Cox had near enough admitted that everything is alright now and we can now leave." Eddy looked at the inspector with a soupcon of hatred and walked out with out saying goodbye.

Outside the building, I endeavored to placate my client, but he was still seething.

---

* Slang for fist

He glanced at me with anger all over his countenance and said, "I don't blame you, Mr. St. John, or that geezer in the office for putting me frew it, but I tell you trufully, I'm gonna find out who did it and before I do anything, even if it costs me money. I'm going to save up all me pony's shit and after I 'ave laid 'em out, I'm going to pour it over 'em bit by bit untul 'ese completely covered 'cos wot he's worf." And with that he stalked off with a determined look on his face and murder in his eyes, and I knew he would do it.

Chapter 11

'D-DAY'

A friend's father had passed away and I naturally attended the funeral and subsequently went back to the House of Mourning for the usual reminiscences of the deceased gentleman and give succour to his widow, daughter and her husband, who were my friends

There was a table groaning with food: cakes, sandwiches and the usual paraphernalia attached to such occasions. There was also drinks of all kinds: brandy, whiskey and gin etc. The friends of the family distributed tea and coffee. I went to collect my tea and sandwiches, which I naturally balanced on each knee as I sat on a high-backed chair, after offering sympathy and general platitudes to all and sundry. I sat studying the assembled congregation. Apart from my friends and the widow, I knew no one. There were young and old, all attired appropriately in somber clothing, except for a young man who was wearing a pullover, frayed jeans and trainers. He was dressed incongruously among the mourners. Relations and friends, I was therefore, curious.

Was he their gardner, window-cleaner or general handyman paying his respects? He interested me, after a while he seemed to pick on most of the elderly relatives and seemed to be talking and comforting the widow.

The daughter of the house and her husband by-passed him without any acknowledgement, and I found this interesting.

As I was sitting in my small world, as apart from Renee, the daughter and her husband Arthur, I knew no one. Then Renee approached me and asked whether I would accompany her upstairs to a bedroom.

As I had had no lunch that day, I intimated that the plate of sandwiches and the tea should follow me and she agreed. I followed her upstairs, balancing my refreshments, and entered the bedroom. Renee indicated that I should sit on the bed as there were no chairs in the room. With trepidation, I sat on the bed, which was so soft that I almost spilt my refreshments, and could have caused havoc in the room, but with dexterity, I managed to hold onto the plate and the cup and saucer.

Renee sat on the other side of the bed looking at me askance, and then she said unnecessarily, I thought, "You know my father has just died."

This said in a House of Mourning, and the tears from her mother and relatives, seemed incongruous. But in her distress I ignored this and she continued. "He had, I suppose you know, a manufacturing dress business, and it is imperative that we keep it going for my mother's benefit."

I nodded sagely, but thought to myself, so what is this to do with me?

"You know of course, that I am a designer and that Arthur has retail experience. We therefore, propose to keep the factory going. Both Arthur and me."

"So?" I asked.

"We want you to help us." She looked at me as if it was not a request, but a demand.

"But you have an accountant for the business," I stated.

"Oh him! I dismissed him just now on the telephone." With that she gave a wave of disdain.

"That is most unprofessional. If you want me to help with the finances of the business, it is incumbent on me to contact him for his permission to take over," I replied.

"Oh pishposh! That's not important now," she said, with an air of frustration.

Incidentally, when one is approached by a new client who has been handled by another accountant, it is professional courtesy to write to the previous accountant, requesting permission to take on the client and request whether there was any objections. The only objection usually is concerned with unpaid fees, but in most cases, permission is readily available and there would be some correspondence and relative information on the client to create a smooth takeover.

Suddenly the door opened, and Arthur walked in. he was a gentleman of the old order, except that he was subservient to Renee. He wasn't, in general terms a foolish person, but in my opinion a complete idiot. He reached his retail managership due to family connections and in the time I had known him, had not added immeasurably to any general conversation on business matters. In fact, he was noticeably silent on that subject and usually on most others. But nevertheless, a nice chap.

"What are you doing, dear?" he enquired of his wife, looking at me with a certain curiosity, as both his wife and I were sitting comfortably on the bed, and fairly close to each other. Not noticing that I was still juggling the plate and cup and saucer.

"I'll tell you later, Arthur. Just go downstairs and leave us alone."

With that Arthur sheepishly left the room, as he did that, the young ill-dressed man walked into the room. Renee looked daggers at him and scowled.

"What do you want?" she asked.

"Sis," he said, with a slight grin on his face. "I just saw Arthur leave and knowing you were on your own with this gentleman," he said, looking at me with a knowing wink. "I thought it best to look after your honour, such as it is."

Renee got up from the bed shaking with anger, shouted at the boy, "Just go, Larry. Don't be as noxious as you are always. This gentleman is a close friend, and a accountant."

I was watching this with interest, and came to the conclusion – after he called Renee 'sis' – that he must be her brother, whom I had never heard of, or existed, as she had never mentioned him.

"No sis, I' not leaving, If you have no liason with this gentleman," pointing at me, "it must be some nefarious dealing which I want to know about." With that, he immediately sat on the floor before us, crossed his legs and looked at us expectantly.

Renee turned to me, still angry over the interruption, and said, "I must reluctantly introduce my brother, Larry, who thank God, lives in Canada, which is still not far enough."

At this, Larry bowed his head in acknowledgement, and said, "Well, sis, what's this all about?"

Renee gave him a hard look, and turned to me saying, "Well, Perry, will you help us?"

Before I could answer, Larry leaned forward and looked at me, and said, "As my sister won't tell me what's going on, perhaps you might, and to relieve your concerns, may I introduce myself to you. My mane is Laurence, Renee's brother, from the Colonies, here to pay my respects to my late father, and to help my mother."

I looked at Renee for guidance, she reluctantly and sharply told her brother what we agreed. He immediately stood up and faced his sister.

"I have a better idea," he stated. "I will take over the business for the benefit of mum. I will run it to two years and will be full-time. Further, I will brook no interference from you or Arthur, and if Perry will accept, the two of us will make a success of it. I must remind you, that I will be in sole charge and any profits will go to mum and no one else. I will stay here with her, take enough salary to my own meager means. Point of fact, I have already discussed this with mum, and she is fully in agreement."

He could have added 'so there', but he didn't and suddenly his demeanour changed, and showed authority, enthusiasm and optimism.

Renee was taken aback. "You've taken the liberty of discussing this with mother without my knowledge. That's just typical of you. You're an egomaniac."

"Sis, you really don't me at all. Do you?"

"Frankly no, I don't wish to."

I was their only audience to witness this sibling rivalry, and was not too comfortable with it, particularly as a) Renee and Arthur were my friends, and b) I seemed to have been reluctantly been placed in the epicenter of this dispute, which frankly I did not understand.

With that both of them left the bedroom and I was left on the bed still holding my plate of sandwiches and tea. I thought to hell with both of them, and finished the sandwiches and drank my tea in silence. As I got up to leave, the door opened again and Larry entered.

"Sorry about the kerfuffle, but I have never got on with Renee. She thinks she is hard working and I'm a wastral. Nevertheless, I meant what I said. With your assistance, I shall carry on the business for exactly two years and this date is not negotiable, and as today 16th July 1968, Whatever the outcome, and hope that my mother will be financially secured. Why am I so hard with Renee is because I know that when the time comes, she will insist on carrying on and I have no interest of doing so, as I have more important things to do back home in Canada."

With that he shook my hand and informed me that he wished to see me at the factory the next morning at 7am.

When I eventually went downstairs to the lounge, I noticed that most of the visitors had left and Larry had his arm around his mother's shoulders and talking to her earnestly. I sidled over to Renee and Arthur, curious to know about the animosity between her and her brother.

I broached the subject and saw Renee give a withering look towards her brother. She then informed that that both her and Arthur were following in their family tradition of working hard and endeavouring to acquire wealth and a certain standing. Whereas Larry was lazy and was a perpetual student.

He was twenty-five years of age and had never done a stroke of work. He had emigrated to Canada to enter university and was still studying for some inexplicable reason. Of course, he seemed to have made a reasonable success of his studies and had a BA and an MA, as far as actual work was concerned, this was an anathema to him.

They could not understand why he had not entered the real world, as they knew it. In fact, they were astounded as to the way he was dressed for the funeral and, in their eyes, showed a disrespect for their father's memory and to all the friends and relatives. In other words, he was a disgrace to all and sundry.

Nevertheless, I liked him, he was unconventional. My impression, after the explanation of his life, was that he was academic, which does of necessity imply that he was intelligent, but not 'worldly wise'.

The next day, as arranged, I reached the factory at 7am, and was greeted by Larry, who had now changed into a suit, shirt and tie. Hair combed and the complete antithesis to our first meeting, I just about recognised this individual. He was not laid-back, but to see him now, he seemed older and more natural. He had taken on – at first glance – the personality of a businessman.

He then informed me that he had already spoken to the staff and explained the situation to them, that he was now in charge. That all questions as to work, was to be directed to him. He was now the boss, the big honcho, and from now on, with their help and co-operation, the business will prosper. Further he will not brook any interference from anyone. The implication being from his sister.

Coincidentally just at the time, the doorbell rang and he went to answer it. Renee and Arthur stood there. Larry looked at them, with an enquiring glance. "Yes?" he asked.

"We're here to see what's going on." Renee replied.

"What do you mean?" Larry requested.

"You know what I mean," Renee answered, and continued, "I and Arthur wish to help." She tried to look past Larry but he moved further towards her to block her view.

"But I don't need you, sis. Although you don't think so, I am capable to run the show for mum's sake."

"You do need me, Larry. I don't think you are capable to continue, and by the way, what is Perry doing here? He's our friend and I would have thought that he would work for me." As this remark, I looked at her with a certain disdain. I had not agreed to work with her but for her! She continued, "I asked him personally to look after dad's affairs and now he seems to be part of your team."

This was a further dig at me and put me in an awkward position. In a way this statement was true and apart from that, she and Arthur, were my friends. Before I could say anything, Larry seemed to relent.

"Alright, sis. You can come into the office, but I must warn you, that you will not discuss anything with any member of staff, and with that proviso, come to the office."

With that we all trooped through the factory, looking straight ahead without any acknowledgement from the staff, entered the small back office. Larry sat in his late father's chair behind the desk. We sat facing at him.

"Sis, I have spoken to the boy and girls in the factory and they are enthusiastic to carry-on as they had great respect for dad. I have promised them a final bonus when we close. As such, I propose now to see our customers and suppliers. I will not explain that I will be closing down in two years, otherwise they may not be interested."

Renee looked daggers at him and said, "Lawrence, tell me my position."

This was an awkward moment, for she was true in her previous statements and apart from that she felt that – although Larry had stated two years – I know she felt that instead of closing the business, she could continue after her brother had left the company.

"Why do you keep on mentioning two years?"

"Because sis, I am going back to university to finish my Ph.D."

"But that's rubbish!" she retorted. "Assuming you make a success, which I doubt very much. You could pass the business to me to continue."

Larry looked at her benevently, and said, "It will be a success under my guidance, I can assure you of that. When I leave – and assuming you took over the business – it would go down the pan and jeopardise mum's inheritance."

Renee looked angry. "I said you were an egomaniac and this confirms it."

Lawrence just gave her a cold look, and said, "When I close the door here, all the stock, machinery and lease will have gone, as such, there will be nothing left for you to do." With that he stood up and said, "I want you to leave now, as I have a lot to do and a meeting with Perry here, and speaking to our lawyers. So goodbye to you." Pointing to Renee and Arthur. He continued with a smile. "I will probably see you at mum's tonight, if I can make it on time." With that he sat, pulled a large pad of paper towards him and began writing.

Renee and Arthur looked at each other in bewilderment. It seemed that both of them did not know what to do. Eventually Renee turned to me, with anger in her eyes.

"You were our friend." She emphasised 'friend'. "It would seem that now you are conspiring with my brother. I now regret ever introducing you to him, as you do not want to back me up." With that withering remark, she went towards the door dragging Arthur with her.

"Renee stop!" I exclaimed. "I am working for your mother's benefit, for the family, including you. It is not a conspiracy. You have a family and cannot spend time in the business. As far as I am concerned, Larry seems to know what he's doing and can spend every hour necessary to do what he promised. I'll be helping in my small way, to benefit everyone and hope that we can still be friends."

Renee grabbed Arthur and flounced out without a backward glance.

Larry looked up from his papers and said to me, "I can't be bothered with that stupidity. I wouldn't take it so much to heart, Perry. She'll come around eventually. If she doesn't, it's no great loss. So lets get down to business." He handed me the notes that he had written and to my surprise, were the most comprehensive proposals and tasks I have ever come across.

The days rolled by. At the beginning I was visiting the factory once a week. Then monthly. The whole place was a hive of activity – orders being placed and manufactured. Money was coming in. The workforce were happy and Larry enjoying it, as he immerse himself in the running of the business.

I saw him socially on occasions, and though there was the original coolness between Renee and me, she realised that the business was being successful, she relented slightly, although there were still tension between her and Larry.

Their mother was trying to reconcile her children and at the same time was delighted, in the fact, that her son was now living at home and working every day.

I reached the factory as normal and did what I had to do. Larry said, "When you're finished we'll go to lunch. I wish to discuss something important with you."

I was intrigued, usually we had sandwiches and tea at work. At lunchtime, Larry and I went to a local restaurant, Larry looked at me, and said, "You know what today is?"

I replied, "Yes, Larry, it's Tuesday."

"No, I don't meant that. Today is one month prior to the two years I said I would run the factory – therefore one year and eleven months to the end. I am now in the process of finalising and closing the factory. Paying redundancy and the bonuses to the staff as promised. Also in the process of selling the stock and machinery. I have spoken to the landlord about returning the lease to them, incidentally they were only too pleased to accept. Finally, I am now working out that all our suppliers are paid and our customers settle their outstanding accounts."

I looked at him over the soup and said, "You're serious, Larry. I frankly didn't believe you when you orignally said it."

"Perry, I told you two years, and I meant it. Mum is now financially secure, as you well know, and that was the object of the exercise. I must get back to Canada, and my normal life."

After the factory was closed, we all gathered at Larry's mother's house. There was of course. Larry, his mother, Renee, Arthur and me. Larry was wearing his torn jeans, the same jersey and dirty trainers – the same outfit that he wore when I had first met him.

Larry stood up as we all sat before him. "Well, folks. I told you two years and it is that now. I know that mum is secure and frankly, there were times I thought I cannot do this. The result is as you all know, was successful, and that was what was important. My work here is done, tomorrow I leave for Canada and back to university. That's the only place where I am truly happy. I would, therefore, like to take this opportunity to thank you, sis and Arthur, and of course, Perry. We have had our differences and originally you weren't too happy with the situation. I sincerely hope that now you realise we did the best for mum. I'm not the wastrel you though I was. There is one important lesson that this has taught me, that is, I never ever want to go into business again."

To the surprise of everyone present, he went to his sister and kissed her, then went upstairs to pack.

We sat there stunned and realised that Larry – although an academic – had hidden talents for entrepreneurship that he would never realise.

SNIPPETS

Chapter 12

REPEATS

Tommy Chapman had been an actor. He could play anything from Ibsen to Coward. Although in truth, Coward and light comedy was his forte'. He could waft across a stage with aplomb. The twitch of an eye, the stance and the voice were all one could appreciate. He had a presence. Unfortunately, the producers or directors did not appreciate this. He was usually kept in the background, the third spear-carrier from the left. This did not deter him and he pressurised and pressed for parts. He even appeared on television! Good Lord! This was in the 1950's when no one watched until the Coronation in 1953. Then the whole country was hooked onto this new medium. The sale of televisions went sky-high, but Tommy had missed his chance. He had one foray on the 'box' and that was that. His one and only showing was entered on his C.V., but the date of his performance was prior to the momentous events of 1953 and therefore, missed by all and sundry. This necessitated a rethink of his profession.

Everyone in the industry knew that only 10% of actors and actresses were working at any one time and Tommy decided – unwisely in my opinion – to seek pastures new. He had been a consummate performer and where then could his talent lay? Of course, in the antique business, where his acting ability could be used to his hearts content. Selling an eighteenth-century pewter jug to a retired Indian Army officer was just a natural extension of his talents. The antique profession opened its welcoming arms to Tommy, whom within a short time had made a success of the venture. Then he telephoned me.

"Perry, darling, can I presume on your time to visit you to discuss an unusual situation apropos my tax position?" he asked.

"Of course, old chap. I would consider it a privilege and an honour," I said calmly, falling in with the vernacular he was used to.

Tommy arrived and sat before me. He carefully placed his homburg* by the side of him, crossed his elegant legs, placed a cigarette in a holder, and lit it, blowing smoke rings. Opening his jacket with a flourish and placing a manicured hand inside with a flourish, he produced an envelope. The whole scene reminded me of a Coward play in the 1930's and I was impressed; I was carried away with the scene and reluctantly held back the temptation to applaud. Good Lord! The public at large had missed an actor of such skill and ability.

"You say, my man, that all income received must be taxed by those blighters. That is true, is it not?" I nodded. "Then old chap, I have a deep confession to make," His eyes were downcast. His pallor changed and he elegantly flicked the ash off his cigarette into the ashtray.

"Really, my good man, surely not." I responded and continued, "You are a pillar of society – a man of correct and upright intentions. I cannot believe this." I felt at that moment I was in an elegant drawing room in a palatial residence,

---

* Hat

overlooking exquisite gardens and Oscar Wilde was putting words into our mouths.

"Sadly it's true, my good fellow. I have not been honest or straightforward concerning my income." I looked at him closely and with certain trepidation as to what was to follow.

With a magnificent flourish he handed me the envelope. I saw that the address was typed with the words 'Private and Confidential' neatly shown at the head of the address.

"As it's private, do I have your assured permission that I may extract its contents?" Tommy nodded sagely and with an elegant flick of the wrist commanded me by gesture, that I had his permission to extract the missive. It was a cheque and letter from a firm of theatrical agents. I read the letter and looked at the cheque. I must admit that I read the letter a number of times and kept on glancing at the amount.

It stated that my client was entitled to a royalty on the TV program he had made and it was a repeat fee. The cheque was for eighteen pence, the fee was for twenty pence, of which the agent had deducted his customary 10% agents fee. Not only that, on glancing at the envelope, I had noticed that it was sent to my client by 'first class' post.

I glanced at Tommy, and he had a grin as wide as the 'Palladium'[*].

"So, old fruit, please inform the men from the ministry of my oversight in not declaring this pittance." He was savouring the delicious moment, his second reward for appearing on this strange new medium at the time. He was revelling in the scene between us.

I told him, "My dear chap, I can't in all honesty inform the Inland Revenue of your unexpected windfall. I know that in the past, mind games have been played between us, but my dear, I

---

[*] Well known theatre in London

cannot go through with your request." Tommy's face changed to a downcast look.

"Oh well, the cheque will, of course, not be banked; I shall, with deep pleasure, frame the note. This will satisfy my desires to reek revenge on that agent, who in all honesty, never appreciated my modest talent." He grinned and then emphasised the word 'Talent'. He continued. "I sincerely hope that by not banking the cheque, his account books will never balance. They will be eighteen pence out."

With that, he took the cheque, letter and envelope and with a slight bow to me, placing his coat over his shoulders, gave me a perfunctory wave and exited my office 'stage left'.

Chapter 13

KEEP A BREAST OF THINGS

Ophelia was a very attractive young lady – petite, slim and vivacious. Her claim to fame was the fact that she had reasonably large mammeries. I can't tell you at this time, the size of her 'shelf', but I believe that they were above normal in ladies of her size and were enhanced and protruded like two ant hills on the meadow of her body. This was therefore, no bad thing. She was the Jayne Mansfield[*] of her time, and English to boot; as such she was noticed. Her talents were limited. She could not dance, sing or act. She was a fixture in anything she did. For this, she was for some reason taken on by a well-known comedian. Perhaps his jokes were ailing. His act was declining, but he must have felt that the introduction of additional interest to his routine would help. At that time it was a stroke of genius, followed later by the likes of the late Benny Hill, who was a genuine and well-loved comedian that could stand on his own, without the introduction of nubile ladies in skimpy clothing.

Her part in the routine was to stand, usually sideways, to show her large accruements, but not saying a word, except to display a smiling exterior. The comedian would enter a routine

---

[*] Famous American actress

whereby he would leer and make certain unsavory jokes. If she was allowed to speak, it could have been a great ventriloquist act with a human dummy. Her first television appearance with the comic caused a sensation. She was hailed as an attractive newcomer and was noticed with abject horror by the professionals, but loved by the public, which was what mattered. Within a fairly short time, she was on other programs, opening bazaars, shops, and making personal appearances. When she was introduced to me to be her accountant, her star was in the ascendancy. Her earnings were considerable, for which she only had to turn up, try desperately to say that so and so was open, smile to the crowd, turn sideways to the audience and photographers, and walk away with a substantial fee. Autographs and photographs were handed out to a willing public. That was all there was to it! Her personality was firmly (if you would pardon the pun) with her breasts.

When news of her appointments with me leaked out – and I never found out who had done that dastardly deed – there would be devoted fans of all ages and sexes screaming "Ophelia' outside my office. During our meetings, I must admit, they were more of a distraction than her well-known assets. I must say that I was tempted to request the Inland Revenue to allow tax relief for depreciation of her assets, as over a period of time I knew, in my innocent way that they would, I assumed, sag and therefore my client's career would be curtailed, if not finished. I discarded the idea, as the Inland Revenue may not take kindly to my request and 'mark my card' accordingly. I felt that to pursue the matter further, I would have to request my client to bare her top, if not her soul, and the illusion might be shattered, for she might have used, perish the thought! Artificial aids... her career did not last longer than five years and I believe that she is now abroad, doing whatever a failed star does.

She was probably the first of many instant stars with just a little bit more than Andy Warhol's 'fifteen minutes of fame'. We are now inundated with boys and girls, men and women, who crave fame with little talent, personality or panache, but Ophelia was the first, and for what I could gather, happy at the time that she was raking in money for nothing, except for what the 'Good Lord' had bestowed on her.

Chapter 14

OFF WITH HIS HEAD

Colonel Spitzer came to me as a client because he was an agent for a particular charity. At the time I thought that to an extent, the work that he was doing was immoral. It was assumed, that when one gave to charity, the bulk of the money collected would be used solely for that purpose. However, some large charities do employ agents for the purpose of collecting donations and for that they receive a commission. Conversely, I suppose that if agents were not employed, less income would be forthcoming. It was a dilemma that Colonel Spitzer appreciated, but as he informed me, he could not find alternative employment.

Colonel Spitzer was born in 1916, and surprising enough, always wished to join the armed forces and tried desperately to achieve his aim. He was accepted eventually by Sandhurst[*], and reached his goal. During the Second World War, he fought in the army and was a career officer. He was also involved in the Korean War and eventually reached the high rank that he held. Then lo and behold, the government in their wisdom made vicious cuts in the Armed Forces budget and offered substantial sums at the time to the officers and lower ranks to leave the

---

[*] Top Military school in England

services. For the officers, this was called 'bowler-hatting', a throw back to the time when most city workers went to work wearing their bowler hats. The government departments dealing with various businesses warned the officers that took the offer, that they should not invest their redundancy funds, one of which was chicken farming, and of course, Colonel Spitzer bought a chicken farm. Whilst in the army, he was adept at the shooting game, but had no business sense.

Of course, he lost his money and as he was unqualified in anything else; the charity work was his only means of earning a living, particularly as he could use his army rank in introductions. Having 'Colonel' before his name on business cards gave him a certain gravitas.

In general conversations between us, I still had my doubts as to his current employment, but I found him interesting, especially because I had an interest in the armed forces. We occasionally went to lunch together and he regaled me with his stories of his army career. I was naturally fascinated with the endeavours that my client and his men went through. The ravages, triumphs and victories, the death and destruction, and above all the heroism of all involved were far more interesting than the mundane conversations I normally had.

One day over lunch, for some reason he opened his heart to me and told me about his secret history. Near the day of his discharge, he was offered a glance at his army file. Apart from the various recommendations and awards that he received, he was shocked and appalled to learn that his father was a Swiss National and living in London at the time of my client's birth – hence his foreign name. Incidentally, Colonel Spitzer did inquire of his mother, who was a widow, as to his antecedents, and was usually quickly brushed off with the fact that although she was English, she had met his father and married him at the beginning of the First World War, and that he had died just after my client's birth from an unspecified illness.

My client had accepted that fact and had not questioned her further. Mr. Spitzer had been arrested by the Security Services for spying for Germany. Further he had been found guilty at his trial and condemned to death. He was executed.

My client's career through the army had not been affected by this incident and although there was this 'black mark' on his file, his progress through the officer ranks had not deterred the authorities from advancing his career to the high rank that he held at the end. When he read the file, he was devastated, however his mother by then had passed away and further information could not be obtained. My client was a supreme patriot to this country and no one throughout his service had hinted at his family past, or even questioned the fact that he had a foreign name. This whole incident had made my client so British that he was now of the opinion that he could carry his name more proudly for what he had achieved, rather than the dastardly deeds of his father. It was pure irony that my client chose to fight for Britain against the works of his father, for the enemy.

Chapter 15

HONOR AMONGST THIEVES

Arnold Brown was a genuine and honest businessman. He was tough, large and strong – a man of imposing demeanour, once seen, never forgotten. His honesty was paramount to him and later, as I found out, to others. To me he seemed a 'pussycat'. Arnold ran his business with the utmost respect amongst his competitors and rivals. His trading was impeccable, his records accurate and he had a charm to 'tempt the birds from the trees'. He was upright and respectable, which to an extent belied his other function. I did not find out about his post-business until much later in our relationship, when he informed me of his past. He told me that where he was born and brought up, the area was unsavoury to say the least. Most of his friends had become criminals – some petty, others major. Arnold himself, for some reason did not enter into any of these adventures and at some time even thought of joining the police force. This was too embarrassing, and if he had, his friends would always be suspicious of him. He would without doubt have been ostracised. Further, he did enjoy the company of his friends. Their enjoyment was symptomatic to their misery.

Because of his utmost honesty, he was trusted and surprisingly treated with a certain respect. He knew and understood their situations, and they knew that whatever they had done criminally, he would not pass judgment. He of course did not approve of physical damage to victims and made his feelings known in no uncertain manner. Fraud, safe-breaking, theft and sundry money scams were acceptable to an extent as long as that was all it was. Any sign of guns, knives, or other weapons were *de rigor* to him, and he told his friends of this quite forcibly. He did not approve of their criminality, but tolerated it. Therefore, because of the trust that they placed in him, he was gradually entrusted with the position of their banker. Not that he actually became a bank, but whilst they were incarcerated they would arrange for Arnie to be able to support their wives and children. He would visit the families and give them money to exist until their spouses or children were released from prison. He never mentioned to me how he obtained the funds, but it was probably from their Ill-gotten gains.

I did not delve into this aspect of his life and as long as he was not getting a declarable income from this source – which he assured me that he did not – I was not interested. When I did occasionally press him on this point and his reasons, I was informed that he felt that he could not see the families suffer for the foibles of their husbands or sons. Furthermore, he enjoyed the company of the families, and upon the release of the offenders, the celebrations were fantastic. He also wallowed in the friendship they offered him, and for the successful criminal who owned property abroad; he was constantly invited to these establishments and was treated as a long-lost friend. Although the bulk of his friendships were with the criminal classes, he did have close relationships with those of a more honest disposition. All these mixed friendships enhanced his life, but he told me that felons were the only people who really enjoyed their lives when it was possible.

One day, Arnold rang me in a bit of a panic. "Mr. St. John, guess what has happened to me?"

I could not guess. I surmised that by his tone, something dramatic must have happened. Arrested? Injured? Smitten by a deadly disease?

"What, Arnie?" I was now very curious.

"I was mugged," he answered, somewhat mournfully.

"You, mugged?" I was incredulous.

"I was coming out of the bank; there was a guy bending down before me and then I was pushed in the back by somebody, and as I fell over the swine bending down, they grabbed my bag of cash and ran off." He was now sounding angry.

"Good Lord! Do you know them or who they are?" I asked. "And did you contact the police?"

"Are you kidding?" he said with venom. "I have been helping the boys in the past and shall naturally put the word out. That's the way we do things."

"I wish you luck," I ventured, but by the sound of the assault, it would seem that the thieves would have run and hidden.

A few days later, Arnie rang me again.

"Hello, Mr. St. John, just to let you know I've my money back and my friendships have come up," he said happily. "They've shown now that they really appreciate what I did for them."

Sometimes, with situations I have gotten myself into, I wished I had friends like that. But then, I do not relish doing the 'Lambeth Walk' or 'Hokey Cokey'* with blowsy women and men with cauliflower ears, and gold bracelets and rings with medallions around their necks.

---

* Cockney songs

Chapter 16

DIVIDENDS

Harry Owen was a retired market trader, but his object in life was two-fold. One was to invest his money in the stock market and beat the stock market index, the second was to pick companies that gave freebies to their shareholders at annual general meetings. Most companies gave a bag of goodies of their products to those that attended the annual meetings. He reached the stage that nearly every day of the week he would attend the company meetings and not say a word. He would, however, leave with a shopping bag full of the companies products. These were his 'perks' and 'rights' as far as Harry was concerned. There were even times when the company would supply coffee, drinks or sandwiches. These were – as far as Harry was concerned – a welcome addition to the 'goodies' and very acceptable.

I never realised throughout our meetings, which over the years he seemed to present to me, documents and dividend warrants which every year seemed to have shown that his wealth had considerably increased. In fact he became a wealthy individual. I had never visited his home, but one day he suggested that I do, and I took up the offer when visiting another client in the area. Harry owned a medium three-bedroom house with the usual mod cons in a North London suburb. When I parked my car, I noticed that his property was different to others in the area, mainly because the garden gate was broken, the path pot-marked by neglect and the front garden a shamble of overgrown grass and weeds. The house looked miserable and the front door was almost paint stripped. It seemed that no money had been spent on the house since it had been built. It was a carbuncle on the body of the street.

My client answered my banging on the door, as there was no bell. He ushered me into the premises and took me straight into the front room. The passageway that I went through had wallpaper peeling from the walls and the ceiling did not contain a light. The front room was also in the same condition, although it did contain an electric bulb of minimum wattage. Harry offered me a deckchair to sit on. There was one other chair in the room, on which my client sat, placed before a card table covered in paperwork. Harry accepted that there was no other furniture in the room. This had not been decorated for some time, although I just gathered this, as the only conceivable decorations on the walls were graphs. These had the names of various companies on them and wiggly lines showing, their particular share prices over periods. These – from what I could see – were meticulously prepared, and my client showed and explained them to me with pride, particularly those companies he had chosen that had beat the stock market share index.

On the floor were cardboard boxes full of brown envelopes, in which were company reports, and more particularly, details of all the 'perks' and 'gifts' that Harry had received. He put his fingers through his braces, which were attached to dirty trousers that were also held up by a belt – the epitome of the perfect 'belt and braces' man. Here was this wealthy man accumulating cash, without any appearance or sign of his vast accumulation. Of course, during our discussions no tea or coffee was offered, but he did offer to take me to lunch in the high street. This I thought must be a first and because of this I accepted with alacrity. As he did not own a vehicle, we left in mine.

When we reached the high street, he suggested that we park near a very expensive restaurant. Why I should be so privileged to be given this largesse from my client? Is he trying to impress me? Does he feel I could do more for him than my usual work? These thoughts were in my mind as I locked the car and walked towards the entrance. I noticed that my client was not following me, but was further down the road. I walked towards him as he entered a 'cheap and cheerful' café. He beckoned me to enter and we sat on a bench before a plastic covered table, on which were used bottles of tomato sauce, saltcellars and vinegar bottles. Harry thrust a menu at me, and with an expansive gesture suggested that I could have any sandwich I desired, together with a mug of tea and that cost was of no consequence. During that period, he seemed to know some of the other diners, who in their forlorn way, flicked the ash of their rolled up cigarettes and gave Harry a perfunctory wave. During my repast, Harry did not eat and I was embarrassed in partaking of my luxuries.

He requested that when we left, would I please drop him at a Pensioners Club where he would have his lunch, as the club was subsidised through the local council and would not cost him more than 50p[*] for a three course meal.

Although Harry was not – at that time – of pensionable age, his poor clothing and general demeanour was acceptable by the authorities as a man of mature age who could not conceivably afford the cost and could not look after himself properly. I left him at the entrance to the club, thinking of the morality of this man, who could conceivably have purchased the property that housed the pensioners and personally subsidised their meals.

---

[*] UK currency 50p = approx. .90c US Dollars

It made me think that 'money is the root of all evil' and the accumulation – in some instances – as with Harry, was an incurable obsession.

Chapter 17

DREAMS – A PART OF THE RICH TRADITION OF LIFE

Tom Oliver was a nice, ordinary chap. He had a reasonable job, wife, three children, a dog, semi-detached[*] house with a mortgage, family saloon car, two weeks holiday a year, shopping trips each week, an occasional cinema trip, and restaurant visits on celebratory occasions. In all senses of the word, he was 'ordinary', and lived a mundane, but reasonably happy life. Of course he had his dreams and interests. Sport was usually paramount in his thoughts when he was younger, but now he had to contend with watching it on TV and indulging in his dreams of glorious victories on the football and cricket pitches, championship wins on the golf course and saluting the checkered flag after winning a grand prix. When all was said and done, motor racing was his ultimate wish to participate in. He knew with his family responsibilities and income this was an impossibility. Motor racing – even rallying – was for young, energetic and wealthy individuals. Not that Tom was old – he was only in his late thirties, but he knew that in his rational moments, his wishes far exceeded his current position. But if a man cannot dream, what then was left for him?

---

[*]British version of a USA Townhome

It was customary for Tom on his lunch break to take his flask[*], sandwiches and newspaper to the square near his office and indulge in his normal rituals of lunching, reading and relaxing before going back to the grind of the office. However, on this particular day, he felt restless and after finishing his sandwiches and emptying the flask, he placed the newspaper, unread, under his arm, looked at his watch and realised he had another half hour before he was due to return to the office. He began walking around the square, and as he did so, he noticed various establishments around the square that he had never particularly noticed before. There, in a car showroom was the most magnificent red sports car – sleek and attractive, full of power, majestically designed, with gleaming headlights, low slung and shiny. The trimmings were pure leather, and the dashboard beautiful, with polished wood. Oh, if only Tom could afford it! Drive it on his own around a race track at speed, wearing a helmet, overalls, with a large number printed on it's side and Tom's name emblazoned down the long, low bonnet. This car was the ultimate. Never mind that it was of foreign manufacture, it epitomised all that Tom could have wished to own in his wildest imagination. Tom stared at the car through the shop window and added to the illusion was the fact that it was the only car on display. As Tom had not seen anything like it before in pictures or magazines, he was indeed curious and entered the showroom to obtain a brochure.

He pushed the glass doors forward, entered and began pacing around the vehicle, looking at it from every angle, taking in its beautiful lines, its newness, the angle of the steering wheel, the chrome of the gear stick and hand brake, and the speedometer that showed a maximum of 180mph. The most important element was the intoxicating smell of the leather and that of Tom's reflection in the shiny body of the vehicle. He mentally drooled over what he saw and felt that come what

---

[*] Hot drink holder

may, he had to have a brochure of the car so he could savour the wish that it could be his.

He turned towards the showroom office, but there was none visible. However, near the back of the shop was a desk seated upon which was a young, elegant man, immaculately dressed, just sitting, swinging his legs and not even glancing at Tom as he approached.

"Excuse me," said Tom, "but have you a brochure to spare of that car that I could have?"

The young man looked at Tom and said in an emphatic tone, "No."

"Why not?" asked Tom. "Every car dealer will give a brochure on any new car".

"Well this one doesn't," said the man.

"That's unusual. Can you give me a reason?" The young man sighed and looked Tom up and down.

"Because you're not suitable." Tom was astonished.

"What do you mean I'm not suitable?"

"I really don't wish to go into it, but I don't think that car is for you."

"Why not?" Tom demanded. "How do you know I'm not suitable?" The young man turned his head away. "Well, answer me!"

The young man turned back to Tom, took a heavy breath and said, "All I can say is that car is not for you. And frankly you are not for that car."

Now Tom was adamant. The man was being off-handed and as far as Tom was concerned, deeply insulting.

"I could easily drive that car. I know how to handle sports cars. I've been motor racing." This was basically a 'white lie'. He had only been a spectator.

"So?" The man said, "I still don't think it's for you." This was making Tom angry.

"Well I do."

The man grinned at Tom. "I'm still not giving you a brochure."

Tom, with a sudden impulse, said, "I don't need the brochure, I'll buy the car."

"If you're sure, I'll get the papers for you to sign." With that, Tom and the salesman completed the documents. On parting the salesman said, "All things being equal, you can pick up the car tomorrow."

Tom went back to work but could not concentrate – he told no one. When he got home, he tried to act normally, ate his food, played with the kids, watched TV and went to bed with his deep secret. That night he tossed and turned, excited but apprehensive. His secret was safe. What a surprise there would be when he drove the car home.

Work the next day was a complete haze, until he entered the showroom. The salesman smiled at him, shook his hand and gave him the keys to his dream. Tom thought 'I'll show them', and with that and a squealing of tires, he drove out of the showroom, almost knocking down a pedestrian and smashing into a passing taxi, with the acceleration that he was not accustomed to.

He drove leisurely home, acknowledging the envious glances of other drivers, feeling like a million dollars. He savoured the look from others and with unprecedented pride, eventually drove up to the drive to his house, and with a loving pat on the bonnet, let himself into the house, where his wife was standing with her customary hands on hips.

"Who lent you that and why?" She demanded. Tom smiled at her.

"It's not borrowed. It's mine."

"Yours?" she screamed.

"Y-y-yes." Tom felt slightly deflated by her tone.

"No, I can't believe it. You're an idiot – just a stupid, bloody maniacal fool."

"Why?" Tom asked apprehensively.

"You have three kids and me and you buy a bloody two seater. You can just keep us in food, clothing and a mortgage. You earn just enough to support us, let alone two cars. You're not a twenty-year-old anymore. Do you want any other reasons? Because if you do, I have many more I can tell you."

Tom spluttered. "I'll find a way."

"What? Rob a bank, put your hand in the till, and murder a rich relative, if we have any. You're stark, staring mad."

"You don't approve then?"

Tom looked out of the window and noticed his children all over the car, and a few neighbours staring in bewilderment.

"Approve? If you want to keep the kids, this house and maybe me, you'll stop all this nonsense and take the damn car back first thing in the morning and get your money back." With that, she stormed out and over her shoulder said, "After you have had your supper in the car, you can sleep in it tonight, as the front door will be locked and will stay so until you come back tomorrow night by your usual bus and prove to me that stupid car has gone."

Tom woke the next morning and stretched himself after sleeping in the car. He realised that he had the best sleep that he ever had and his dream during the night of racing his car against all-comers and winning wreaths and cups made up for all his wishes and dreams – if only for a few hours – until he gave the car back to the dealership.

When he did, the salesman gave him a look of 'I told you so', but Tom's dream had come true, and from then on he was mentally satisfied that dreams in part can come true, if only for a fleeting moment.

Chapter 18

LATE-NT FEAR

Or That which shapes us forever

The client that sits in front of our imposing desks, looks upon us as a person without fear and trepidation – a leader, and professional that will lead them forward into all situations, thwarting any adversity that comes before them. Little do they realise that even accountants, yes, even accountants can have fears that have shaped our very being, ingrained forever into our psyche.

I'm not a great fan of psychiatry or psychologists. I do not understand the mind, neither, I suspect, do those who practice it. In fact, there was an old maxim that psychiatrists should have their brain examined. Fortunately, I have never met or consulted any of its eminent members. Nevertheless, I do have one particular fear, and that is being late for meetings, appointments, missing trains and planes, or anything that purports to time and date. I have spent more time reading five-year-old magazines in doctor's and dentists surgeries. I have twiddled my thumbs for half an hour before meeting someone, being looked at suspiciously, as I have paced up and down outside a building, ages before going to meet somebody. I have been known to throw tantrums if a person I was meeting was late. I perspire and shake during this waiting period. Insane thoughts enter my head until the allotted time.

I had arranged a meeting with clients in the country and therefore had to catch a train at 9.15am. My clerk was going to accompany me. I was sitting in the train carriage at 8.30am. My clerk had not arrived! I tried to read a book, but could not concentrate. By 9am I was wiping my brow with my handkerchief and looking out of the window. At 9.13am I was in a faint. My clerk had not arrived! I leaned out of the window as the guards began blowing whistles and waving flags. I then saw him running along the platform towards me. He opened the door into my compartment, seconds before the train began its slow journey away.

There was no apology. When I screamed at him that he was late and got into a manic paddy*, he just looked at me with a disdainful look and self assurance, "I caught the train, sir, didn't I?" That was it!

I could have pummelled him to a pulp, poked his eyes out with my Biro and swore at him continuously. I did nothing, except not speak to him for the rest of the two and a half hour trip.

But what is this all about?

We are now reaching the crux of my fears. Which I assume has the basis of my abject hatred of lateness. We are back with the trains. I must have been about nine-year-old, and my parents were taking me on our annual vacation for a week at the coast for pleasure and freedom. The three of us had settled in the carriage, when my late father stated that he wished for a cup of tea. There was no restaurant car on the train, but along the platform there was a barrow selling drinks. I was therefore instructed to go and buy the tea, which I did and gave it to him.

---

* Argument

174

He took the first sip and spluttered, "There is no sugar" I was duly dispatched to the barrow for sugar.

When I returned, my father put the white substance into his tea and took a further sip. He spluttered, "This is salt!" I returned again to the barrow and by now there was a queue* growing, and I waited patiently to be served. Then the whistles blew and the flags waved and the train began its movement.

My dear mother was leaning out of the window, screaming at me to hurry. I ran to the carriage, but in those days the doors automatically locked and of course I could not get in. Fortunately the train guard grabbed me as the train passed and pulled me into his van at the rear. He then escorted me along the corridor to my parent's compartment. I was still holding the sugar, which I gave to my father. His tea, by now, was cold, but this was forgotten during my mother's crying, and cuddling me as if I had emigrated to a far-off land and just returned – although it had only been a few minutes of absence. I was excited at the incident and took that as part of life's rich tapestry.

During the vacation, my parents, in order to please me decided on a boat-trip. This was duly booked for the afternoon and we went to a local restaurant in town for a light lunch, as we were unsure of my mother's sea legs and did not wish to be embarrassed by the lunch returning out to sea. The boat anchored off the pier was large, with funnels and paddles and quite a number of passengers vying for seats where they could view the water and catch the sun's rays. We stepped on deck and found seats at the rear. My mother then enquired where my blazer† was. I gave her a blank stare, as in those days, even to the present day, I was not particularly sartorially aware.

---

*People standing in line
† Jacket

My mother, with a tinge of anger, stated that I must have left it at the restaurant and instructed my father to go into town and retrieve it. He reluctantly left the ship, after giving me a withering look.

After what seemed an age, he had not returned, to my mother's consternation. I was blissfully unaware of her concerns, as I was below decks putting my hands into the sea and trying to catch any passing fish. The klaxons on the ship began bellowing their mournful tune. The sailors became active and the passengers were settling down to a pleasant sea journey. The sailors were getting ready to remove the gangplank and hawsers preparatory to sailing and I rushed on deck to see my mother rushing forward to the captain, explaining the position concerning my father's non attendance.

The captain announced his concern, but stated that the ship had to catch the tide and could not wait. My mother was in complete panic and begged with him to wait, but with at least five hundred passengers on board who had already paid for the trip, the captain wasn't particularly interested and even suggested that both my mother and I vacate the vessel. I was standing in the stern of the ship looking towards the town, and then I saw my father running towards us along the pier, carrying what looked like a bundle of rags under his arm. The gangplank had been pulled up; the ship was steadily moving away. I was excited and shouting to my father to hurry. My mother was beside herself and in tears and the captain was showing no concern.

My father, at the time being quite young and fit, reached the side of the boat, which was now five feet away from the pier, and took an almighty leap and landed on deck. All the passengers were cheering and my father, with a certain aplomb, handed the blazer to me and stated, without losing breath, "I believe this is yours, son," as he handed me the garment.

My mother fell upon him laughing, crying and cuddling both of us in complete delirium. With all that commotion, she forgot about her lunch and kept it down. The trip was fine, the holiday excellent, with no more alarms and excursions.

Now you understand my fear. I suppose on reflection, there is something in this psychological clap-trap, but where does my fear of insects come from? Of course I wished over the years to combat my concerns regarding 'time'. If only I did not suffer! I crave the *joi de vivre* of the latecomer – the excuses that can be given for being late, or the ingenuity of lateness at a meeting and "drumming-up" an excuse, however bizarre. The thought out intelligence and downright lie given for not being on time. Oh! How I wish I could, with straight face, give an outlandish reason for not being on time. 'Excuse liar', how I envy your panache and inventiveness.

SUMMARY

The heading of this chapter, in my opinion, is a stroke of genius, as accountants must be good at 'sums'. In school, those pupils that had a leaning towards mathematics were either guided towards sciences or to the profession. The basis of accountancy is the ability to work with figures – to understand the intricacies of the result of numbers. The age-old method of adding up a column of numbers from top to bottom and then from bottom to top to see that their totals agree was expected and accepted. To look at an account book with lots of numbers to be totalled seemed formidable, and to most, mind-blowing. A more daunting prospect and boring task one could not imagine, but it had to be done. In my own case, I played mental games with the figures. It was amazing how many times particular numbers would occur. Prior to decimalisation, there were three columns of figures for pounds, shillings and pence[*], and therefore you would not only have to add the columns, but use divisions mathematics to bring them to order – as between pence, shillings and then into pounds.

I will not bore you with the fact that there also was fractions of pence involved. Suffice to say it was number-crunching on a big scale, but this mental skill was eventually taken over by calculators. I didn't particularly take to this new

---

[*] UK Currency replaced in the 1970's with the existing currency

invention except as a Godsend for intricate mathematical calculations for percentages, etc. I felt that it was imperative that the calculator gave a print out that one could check. Fortunately the calculator could not, in reality, be wrong. It was the operator. To enter, for example, the figure of £24.84 as £248.40 and therefore assume that the total displayed is correct, can throw the whole calculation into chaos.

The display is correct, but the totals wrong, thus the mathematics that forms the basis of the profession is paramount. There was a case a number of years ago concerning fraud, and when the senior partner of a leading firm of accountants was in the dock[*] as a witness, a senior barrister asked him whether the figures on the balance sheet that his firm had prepared, were equal, as they should be. The witness took umbrage at the request to add up the figures. However, on insistence, he did and 'shock of shocks' they did not add up correctly… an embarrassing moment.

Out of curiosity, most people who receive accounts either from clubs or companies or their own, do mentally add up the figures to try to catch out the auditors, treasurers or whoever prepared them. If they do not agree, one could always blame the printers or those that typed them originally, if errors are found. It is a curious profession. We use what is known as the 'historical convention'. In other words, we are dealing with figures and accounts, which by date have passed. You could say, in one respect, we are acting as pathologists. We are working on dead numbers, but so much credence is placed on them that it becomes important. They may show cyclical trends – they could also show gradual declines and upward mobility. However, their study is 'crystal gazing'. Therefore, although mathematics is an integral part, accountancy is an art, although the basic tools are a science.

---

[*] British term for 'witness box'

Accountants are now proliferating in all forms of government, industry and commerce. They are considered an essential cog in the wheel. The groovy term now is 'bottom line'. The surplus, the profit, the accumulation of funds is now of extreme importance and essential in every aspect of life.

Those that handle the finance are revered for some reason. That is why the Chancellor of the Exchequer lives next door to the Prime Minister. Perhaps the Prime Minister pops next door to ask for change from a tenner[*]. This shows the importance of that high office. With banks and finance houses, building societies dealing with millions of pounds, the average individual cannot comprehend these sums. They are just figures, seemingly snatched from the ether.

Many years ago, Sam Snead, a famous American golfer, won a tournament and the sponsors presented him with a cheque for his winnings. He could not comprehend the amount and demanded that they paid him in cash – not notes, but coins. They acceded with his request and he eventually took away his winnings in a wheelbarrow. That way he could actually see the money and appreciate it.

Continuously having had to deal with money in all its aspects has become somewhat abhorrent to me, and I have no interest in the ramifications of my own finances. I also suppose that I cannot pay fees to anyone for looking after my own. To most people, this attitude is bordering on the immoral. I had found over the years, talking to clients, that the dearest thing next to their hearts was their money. Therefore, once they had unburdened themselves of this secret, everything else was secondary. I then found out, whose son was a drug addict, whose daughter was on 'the game'[†], the name of my client's mistress and which wife was having an affair.

---

[*] British slang for £10.00 in cash
[†] Prostitute

This brings us to the most important aspect of the accountant's practice, and that is the client. They come in all forms and sexes – in fact, sometimes more than the two sexes.

They are fat and thin, tall and short, wealthy and on the verge of penury, clever and ignorant, bosses and workers. In fact, the whole gamut of life is there. This is why accountancy is interesting, boring, exciting, spontaneous and deliberating. It's also continuous, as even after death, we are still involved in what is known commonly as 'death duties'. Thus our work for our clients is never done. That is until the estate is collected and distributed and the undertaker is satisfied, the tombstone is erected and the file is interred. Then, and only then, can we sit back with a mournful smile on our faces, knowing that we have done our best for our clients through their working lives and their eventual passing. Their memorial is that they have done their best during their stay, to satisfy themselves, their families and the government – what better than to quote 'our lives were reasonably normal and we have complied with all our obligations, and satisfied our responsibilities'.

FINAL THOUGHTS

I am a reasonable man. Fairly bright, fairly educated, fairly tidy, fairly short in stature, fairly content, fairly knowledgeable, fairly charitable, fairly cowardly, fairly smart, fairly understanding, fairly old, fairly placid.

BUT with all that, I am annoyed at government. Since the Halcyon days of yore, of which I have written, there has been considerable change. The government, in their wisdom – and to show to the citizens that it is in control of your money – have combined the efforts of the Inland Revenue and Customs & Excise into one entity and have called it 'HMRC' – Her Majesty's Revenue and Customs, in order to save us taxpayers further contributions to their coffers. However to telephone them for any enquiry, they now use an '0845' prefix which is above the normal rate of a telephone call, added to which they start with a preamble informing us good people that our calls are monitored for training purposes, thus extending the length of the call. My response is when I get through to them eventually, I repeat the same mantra just to even things up.

Of course technology now has to take over – the tasks previously used in offices and now everyone is available '24/7'. Where did we go wrong? It must have been the pursuit of leisure that was our undoing, during the time when the UK ruled the world, our trading was buoyant and we were masters of all we surveyed. It was realised that we had it too easy and had to be divested of our pursuits and settle down to what is serious business, whether we wanted to or not.

Office workers now believe that 'Apple' and 'Blackberry' are part of their essential five-a-day fruit and vegetables. All I can say is that now I have a computer (Lord help me) I use it near an open window, for when I throw it out in frustration, I will not be covered in shards of glass.

SUCH IS PROGRESS.